Crazy World

Gender, sexual politics and the faithful church

John Benton

Dr John Benton is Director of Pastoral Support with the Pastors' Academy at London Seminary

Crazy World

Gender, sexual politics and the faithful church

John Benton

Grace
Publications

Grace Publications Trust
62 Bride Street
London N7 8AZ

www.gracepublications.co.uk

First published in Great Britain by Grace Publications Trust 2023

Cover design by Pete Barnsley (CreativeHoot.com)

A record for this book is available from the British Library.

ISBN Paperback: 978-1-912154-78-4
ISBN Ebook: 978-1-912154-80-7

Printed and bound in Great Britain by Ashfords Colour Press

Contents

Part Four: Gender Confusion

A briefing for Bible Christians

Foreword

Our society is in pain. Families are breaking down and individuals are suffering. Much of this is caused by the fact that Christian sexual ethics have been jettisoned as archaic and oppressive. While holding to biblical truth, the church needs to be both compassionate and understanding in order to try to direct people aright.

Rather than compromise with a confused and misled secular culture, the church must do some thinking.

This book does not pretend to have all the answers. But hopefully it does contain some worthwhile insights. It is a compendium of four booklets written across 2018 to 2022. They are titled, *Atheism, Gender and Self-harm*; *Lovers of themselves*; *Soft Totalitarianism* and *Gender Confusion*.

The first was written for the 2018 conference of the Council for Biblical Manhood and Womanhood UK at the Angel Church, Islington, London. But I began thinking about this subject partly because I became aware of young women who were church attenders and had made a Christian commitment, who were secretly self-harming.

The second, *Lovers of themselves*, starts with a biblical introduction to the atheistic outlook of today's world and then goes on to give a basic précis of Carl Trueman's excellent volume *The Rise and Triumph of the Modern Self*. Trueman's work is a Christian view of the sexual revolution and should be read by every pastor. But being a large book many church leaders will find they don't have the time – hence the précis.

The third part, *Soft Totalitarianism*, seeks to explain how, hand in hand with the sexual revolution, political correctness, though perhaps well-meaning, has turned into an oppressive philosophy which may well threaten the future of churches faithful to the Bible.

The fourth, *Gender Confusion*, is an expanded version of a talk given at the Annual Meetings of the Association of Grace Baptist Churches (South East) in October 2022. In writing this I am extremely indebted to my friend Ruth Woodcraft who has furnished me with the results of much of her research into this subject. Some of the contents overlap with my brief work *The Woke Agenda: a guide for pastors*.

Together, these four extended essays in book form will hopefully be a help to busy pastors and leaders as they seek to shepherd their flocks in what has become a crazy world.

John Benton
Director for Pastoral Support Pastors' Academy
London Seminary

Part One:
Atheism, Gender and Self-harm

Introduction

In the Western world at the present time, many young males are committing suicide. Also young females are self-harming at an alarming rate.

This material started as an attempt to understand this twenty-first century tragedy from a biblical point of view. It may not be possible to completely get a handle on it – but this hopefully provides a worthwhile line of thought concerning what is going on.

On our shelves at home we have a copy of *The Dangerous Book for Boys*. It is a large hardback and consists of a collation of fact and fiction, prose and poetry, traditionally of interest to boys. These are things like Rudyard Kipling's poem 'If', the battles of Lord Nelson, the story of Scott of the Antarctic, how to navigate by the stars etc. It is about adventures and achievements in 'touch and go' situations. It is about fights and courage and chivalry.

Next to it we also have the equally large *Daring Book for Girls*. This is not quite the same – but again there is lots of adventure, risk taking and brave women. It includes the stories of people like Florence Nightingale and Amy Johnson, the first female pilot to fly alone from Britain to Australia.

There is a part in us all that responds – especially for men, but for women also – to these things. There is something in us which relishes 'the good fight'. Humanity seems made for a life of contending, of conflict, of striving for something better, of taking on the opposition and winning through. It is as if we were made with a necessity to find our significance as people through a worthwhile battle story. And that story we are able to tell ourselves about ourselves is very close to our deepest identity, our very self.

The story we see ourselves as living gives us meaning and purpose in life. If what we think of ourselves at the deepest level undergoes radical damage and disruption, our lives begin to fall apart.

1. Humanity according to Scripture

Where does that sense of fight and the need to achieve come from? Is it just a vestige of the battle for survival inherited from our (supposed) evolution and which needs to be discarded in the modern world? Or, changing worldviews, from a Christian standpoint is it something sinful? Is contending inherently wrong-headed as some would have us believe?

The story that we tell ourselves about ourselves invariably involves an element of battle. Our lives are about winning through in a diffcult world. I want to argue that this has a proper place in a well-rounded humanity. But I also want to trace how it is subverted, misdirected by sin and so is ruining many lives. This ruination invades every area of our reality including our gender and our very humanity.

Contending

Secularism asks all the right questions, but comes up with all the wrong answers. To understand ourselves we need to go back to the Bible book of Genesis and our creation by God.

Let's see seven things about who we are.

1. *Human beings, male and female, are made in the image of God.*

> Then God said, "Let us make mankind in our image, in our likeness ... So God created mankind in his own image, in the image of God he created them; male and female he created them (Gen. 1:26–27).

Men and women both have the astonishing privilege of God himself being the blueprint on which we are patterned. So there is a sense in which men and women are the same (don't be surprised that girls can be adventurous too). But of course, we are different as well. Just as there is equality, but unity and diversity within the Trinity (Father, Son and Holy Spirit) – so we find the same in humanity at creation.

2. *The work that God gave us involves multiplying and subduing.*

> God blessed them and said to them, "Be fruitful and increase in number; fill the earth and subdue it. Rule over the fish in the sea and the birds in the sky and over every living creature that moves on the ground" (Gen. 1:28).

This project, which God sets before Adam and Eve, involves not just multiplying, but conflict. They are to 'subdue' the earth – not to exploit it – but to bring it under their rule and so to fruition. The original word here translated 'subdue' is the word often used in the Old Testament for victory in a battle. For example, Zechariah 9:15 speaks of overcoming (or subduing) with sling-stones. The word is used of Israel's conquest of the Promised Land under Joshua (Num. 32:22,29; Josh. 18:1). So this task which God set at the beginning for humanity involves taking on the wilderness ('wildness'). It was to be conquered – civilized. There is a contending for something better. This was to be, under God, our story.

3. The conflict for which we were made is outside the garden.

Genesis 2 explains this in a more detail. Man himself is made out of the dust (Gen. 2:7) and then God puts him into the bit of the world which he has already subdued and made fruitful – the garden of Eden (Gen. 2:8). So the garden was a safe place, a place to meet with God (and therefore a temple), but also something of a first example. Adam is to subdue the earth and this is what it can look like. (We are reminded of the old *Blue Peter* TV children's programme where the presenters would often be showing viewers how to build something and say, 'Here's one I made earlier'). So right from the beginning, even without the Fall, it seems there was a proper sense in which God expected Adam to go outside the garden into the wild to 'fight' to extend Eden across the earth. This is the task, the adventure, the conflict for which we were made. It seems to parallel God's bringing order out of the earth's original darkness and formlessness (Gen. 1:2).

4. Eve is made to help Adam in the task.

> The LORD God said, "It is not good for the man to be alone. I will make a helper suitable for him" (Gen. 2:18).

The designation 'helper' implies no denigration of the woman for it is a term used of God himself, for example in Psalm 46:1. The woman is to be man's companion in the task. She is made from him, understanding him, socializing him, complementing him; not just helping *him* per se, but helping him in the context of the work they carry out for God. Adam first of all is in the garden alone so he becomes the pioneer/ leader. Eve comes after, alongside him. So if his task involves a fight it is not unfeminine but part of true femininity for a woman to be capable of fighting. And you will soon see that rightly if you touch her children, or perhaps even the reputation of her man.[1]

5. Though men and women are equally made in God's image, they are different.

Based on Genesis 2 – without going into details – masculinity has relatively pronounced features of work, leadership, strength to sacrifice. Femininity is relatively pronounced along the lines of help, people skills (harmonizing, team building) and sensitivity. I must emphasize the 'relativity' of this reality because we get into diffculties if we make things too black and white, for example, if we say men can't be sensitive or women can't be sacrificial. Of course we can because we are both human. But the way male and female are made means that we generally exhibit certain features more prominently.

6. All this was originally to take place under the loving Fatherhood of God and in a relationship of trust in him and working for his glory.

The Lord God, in one sense, is the 'audience' watching over all that is done. It is before him that mankind's achievements take place. Made in his image and carrying out his will, imparts true significance to Adam and Eve's lives.

---

1   I have highlighted the contending, 'made for a conflict', aspect of our original humanity. So immediately I want to say that, unlike the risk-averse outlook, a biblical understanding acknowledges that risk taking and a fight for the better, has a legitimate place in our humanity. It is there for both men and women – though especially for men. Courage and contending are rightly part of us. Life is not all about health and safety.

7. But now it is essential to note the way that those aspects of who we are have been subverted and misdirected by the Fall.

Lured by Satan's deception, 'you will be like God', determining for themselves what is good and evil' (Gen. 3:5, my paraphrase), Adam and Eve fall. They step way beyond the bounds set by God, and become rebels against their Creator. The Fall brings many terrible consequences because of God's judgment. But what changes in the area of contending?

First, can I put it like this – whereas before they would have been contending for God – to see the world subdued for his glory – now that competitiveness becomes self-centred. Their choice to disobey God was self-centred – think of yourself – 'you will be like God' (Gen. 3:5). Therefore, the whole of our psychology becomes self oriented.

Second, our opponent changes from a wild world, to Satan and his seed. To Satan God says, 'I will put enmity between you and the woman, and between your offspring and hers' (Gen. 3:15). This then flows over into a prophecy of the Saviour, our Lord Jesus Christ, 'he will crush your head and you will strike his heel.' Satan, this new opponent of mankind, who usurps power over the world, is far too powerful for us. Without the Saviour we must be losers.

Third, following the Fall, excluding God from the picture, in our minds, the audience of our lives mostly changes to ourselves, and what other people think of us. (Perhaps here are the roots of celebrity culture).

So hatred, injustice and selfish ambition break upon the world. Amidst all this there is what the apostle Paul calls 'the good fight' – against evil. But in every area of life there is selfish conflict. The part of us which has 'fight' in it, has been subverted. But for the purposes of our subject, I want to just flag up how conflict has entered in the area of gender and who we are as human beings.

2. Male and female in conflict with each other

Since the Fall the genders made for harmony and unity in diversity (Gen. 2:24) are now pitted against each other. This emerges first when the man blames the woman (and hence God) for his disobedience (Gen. 3:11–12) and then in God's judgment on the woman, 'To the woman he said ... Your desire will be for your husband, and he will rule over you' (Gen. 3:16). The word 'desire' is the same as that used of sin's desire to control or enslave Cain (Gen. 4:7). And sadly, in response the man will seek to rule, or 'lord it' over the woman like a king. This gender conflict is not always of the same intensity and has historically gone through many sad and damaging stages. But at present it manifests itself in that the Western world has become, in a sense, anti-male.

Anti-male culture

I first became aware of this some years ago as my wife and I watched a TV police drama series about two women detectives. It was called *Scott & Bailey*. As I watched this over the weeks I realized that every male character in the show was either deviously nasty or an idiot. It occurred to me that if a TV series had portrayed women like that there would have been uproar. But, somehow, to do that to men was okay.

What are we to make of this? Where has it come from? Here are a few ideas. I'm using Jordan Petersen a little here. He is the Canadian Professor of Psychology who has become something of a YouTube phenomenon with his articulate and outspoken resistance to much of the prevailing political correctness. He has much to say about masculinity in his book 12 *Rules for Life – an antidote to chaos*.[2] He is not a Christian, but has much very insightful common sense.

He says, 'Boys are suffering in the modern world'. Let me paraphrase how he argues this. Boys have always tended to be more disobedient, more independent. He says, 'Boys tilt towards things; girls interests tilt towards people' (p298). That's no surprise to us biblically. These differences are evidently more pronounced in societies, like Sweden, where gender-equality is pushed hardest. The reason this is cited is because it is the opposite of what is expected by those who insist that gender is a social construct. It isn't. The facts say 'No'. The evidence of research is against it. Again biblically we are not surprised. God made the two genders (Mt 19:4).

With a heightened desire for a fight, boys like competition especially as they feel the need in adolescence to strive for independence. They want to be their own person, be someone in their own right and escape the shadow of mum and dad – even if it is as a nerdy computer geek who can outstrip mum and dad at all things social media, digital and online. In a fallen world, this attitude of boys has often been a problem for society. They need to prove themselves.

2   Jordan B Petersen, 12 *Rules for Life: an antidote to the chaos*, Allen Lane Publishing, 2018

The secular confusion

But now, as we have become more intentionally secular/atheist as a society it has led to a situation in which, it seems, boys can never win. That's how Jordan Petersen puts it.

Society's thinking has changed profoundly in recent decades. And the atheist/secular explanation of humanity brings with it an inherent contradiction which damns men.

In the area of being of course, everything is explained by godless, chance, evolution. But a hierarchy is innate to the concept of evolution. It works via survival of the fittest. The fittest = stronger = better. Because men are naturally stronger than women this inevitably (on the logic of evolution alone) leads to a male dominance/ patriarchal society. I'm not defending the misuse of male power; I'm just noting the fact of male power and the way it is explicable in secular evolutionary terms.

In the area of behaviour things are different. In strict chance evolution there is no morality. All that prevails is 'might is right'. So, for example, in his recent best-selling book *Sapiens*, which proposes a thorough atheistic explanation of life, Yuval Haran comments on the US Declaration of Independence.[3] The Declaration famously speaks of holding equality and certain rights for individuals as self-evident. Haran dismisses it saying simply 'there are no such things as rights in biology' (p123).

But with our God-given humanity seeping through, generally, human beings can't stomach such hard-headedness. So the nearest thing to morality which might vaguely have some logic to it is equality. We are all human beings, we are all the same and so justice = equality. (Obviously this has some resonance with Marxism).

---

3   Yuval Noah Haran, *Sapiens: a brief history of human kind*, Harper-Collins, 2011

But step back a moment. There are these two explanations in the areas of being and behaviour. Here's the contradiction; equality doesn't fit with evolution, which is innately hierarchical. Why would the strongest want to work for equality?

And further, evolution doesn't work with equality. It works by 'survival of the fittest' and fittest means 'not equal'. So our society has this inner contradiction. And with these two contradictory sets of logic in play, the male of the human species finds he is inevitably condemned.

From the equality mindset, to use power to advantage yourself over others is to be oppressive. Men are accused of misusing strength (which of course as sinners, biblically speaking, many men sadly have done) to dominate women. And women claim victim status.

This means that many secular men feel they can never win or be the hero of their story. The conclusions are as follows:

a) If men win in competition with women equality says they are being oppressive.
b) If a man uses his strength to help women equality says he is being condescending and patronizing.
c) If a man loses to a woman, evolution says he is a wimp.

Putting this all together takes us back to Scott & Bailey (and Peppa Pig). All men are either evil or idiots to be despised. And therefore

d) If women are to gain equality men must be positively discriminated against because they are generally more powerful creatures.

Boys are in trouble

So much has this form of thinking prevailed that Jordan Petersen writes:

> There are whole disciplines in universities forthrightly hostile towards men. These are areas of study dominated by the post-modern/neo-Marxist claim that Western culture, in particular, is an oppressive structure, created by white men to dominate and exclude women (and other select groups); successful only because of that domination and exclusion.[4]

What we learn is this: If you move away from a biblical world view of the complementarity of men and women, 'boys are in trouble.' Thus it happens that many a male's estimate of himself sags. He feels 'I'm a loser' whichever way he turns. There will naturally be other factors involved once we start considering individual cases. These push in the same direction and influence the high rate of male suicides. Perhaps it is poverty or lack of opportunity. But it is clear that the underlying anti-male outlook will feed in to even those areas too for many men.

So we have young men who believe that they can never live a significant life (especially as, in a secular world, other people are the audience and give significance, not God). They feel condemned just for being male. This feeling of never being acceptable will be amplified by the particularities of a young man's own situation. For example, there might be an especially distressing break-up of a relationship or a brutal dismissal from the workplace. In the story of their life they can never win. They succumb to self-loathing and many to suicide.

The corollaries of this anti-male tendency should also be noted:

---

4   Jordan B Petersen, 12 *Rules for Life: an antidote to the chaos*, Allen Lane Publishing, 2018, page 302

- Female mentality becomes the norm. Masculinity is dominant, abnormal – problematic
- Also it means that traditional femininity declines. Women must reach 'the top' which has previously been defined by male pursuits. Therefore, to be a successful woman is to do what men have done traditionally. So being a mother, not a wage earner, is to be a failure as a woman.

This is how the gender conflict works out. But the impossibility of winning goes deeper.

3. The individual against himself/herself

In 2 Timothy 3, Paul introduces us to the terrible times that can occur during 'last days' in godless society. Here are his words:

> But mark this: there will be terrible times in the last days. People will be lovers of themselves, lovers of money, boastful, proud, abusive, disobedient to their parents, ungrateful, unholy, without love, unforgiving, slanderous, without self-control, brutal, not lovers of the good, treacherous, rash, conceited, lovers of pleasure rather than lovers of God – having a form of godliness but denying its power (2 Tim. 3:1-5).

Notice his headline. People will be lovers of themselves. What we love is our god. Self becomes god. Self is worshipped. We sacrifice everything else for the self. Freedom is self-determination. It's not diffcult to see that that's where we currently are in Western society.

Sacrificing all else to self

Feminism from 1960–1990 moved away from the proper call for women's voices to be heard and votes to be given to women, themes that characterized earlier feminism. In this era, feminism was set in terms of liberation for women. The agenda was as follows:

- Women to be liberated from marriage, motherhood and housekeeping
- Women to be liberated from family life – abolish patriarchy

- Women to be liberated from reproductive function
- Women to be liberated from old fashioned morals
- Women to be liberated from 'heteronormativity' – that is male and female as the norm for relationships
- Women to be liberated from patriarchal religion.[5]

It all tends in one direction – the 'setting free' of the 'self'. Everything is sacrificed for 'self'. Family, motherhood, even right and wrong must go. Then, and only then, would there be freedom for women.

And, of course, this wasn't just the agenda for women but in many ways was the whole direction of society – and still is. Where did this whole direction come from?

A history of how we see the self

We need to look at 'the self' and how we view it. Will Storr's 2017 book *Selfie: How the West became Self-obsessed* gives his take on what has been unfolding, especially over the last century or so. It is worth considering. [6] Let me try to give a summary of his thesis.

With the rejection of our Christian heritage, say in the mid-nineteenth century, and embracing of secularism, our view of the self began to change. Storr calls the Christian view 'the bad self'. Sadly he has a very limited view of what Christian faith teaches, but he has rightly picked up on the fact that we are sinners. Setting aside that human beings are gloriously made in God's image, but now are fallen, deeply flawed and in need of redemption through the love of God in Christ, into the emerging secular world came Freud with his

---

5 I am indebted to Sharon James for these headings.

6 Will Storr, *Selfie: how the West became self-obsessed*, Picador, 2017

ideas of the subconscious based on Greek Myths. But he was still proposing that the heart of the self was dark and twisted.

I am skating over a great deal here, but to cut a long story short, Freud's ideas proved too gloomy for modern people. They were replaced with a theory of 'the good self'. That deep-down human beings are good. We are only messed up by our experiences. Popular psychology was born.

Then, during the mid-twentieth century this 'good self' began to be pushed a little further into what Storr titles, 'the special self.' Not only are we basically good, but if we would only understand how special we are, build our self-esteem, human beings would know true fulfilment.

It is interesting that around this time, 1980s-1990s, the names of Western children begin to change. Peter and Susan, Janet and John fell out of fashion. Parents began to go for unusual names. They began to try to choose names which were unique to their child such as Madison or Tuesday. I have even come across a child named Zeus – the chief deity of mythology. Mothers and fathers wanted their children to have names which said, 'You are special – stand out and be a star'.

California and self-esteem

Again I am condensing things hugely here, but Storr highlights what he sees as a particular turning point. Based somewhat on the ideas of the psychologist Carl Rogers, back in 1987, a man named John Vasconcellos, was given permission to form a state financed 'Self-Esteem Task Force' in California. He believed that by raising self-esteem you could solve a massive array of chronic social problems. Crime, violence, educational failure, teenaged pregnancy, drug and alcohol abuse would disappear if people only realized how special they are.

Support for this project was sought. A spokesman for a group of academics from the University of California aided Vasconcellos' cause. The word went out from a press conference along the lines of 'Research proves that this approach is right'. This news proved crucial. The experts had proved it. From there a gargantuan 'self-esteem' movement really took off and is now worldwide. The whole of political correctness followed in its wake – not damaging a minority's self-esteem must be a priority above all else. This now, more or less, rules the Western world.

But there is a problem. Storr's book is just one of many which have now exposed the fact that the report of the academics' support was not true. [7] It was a blatant misrepresentation. The back story seems to be that, in fact, Vasconcellos held some of the purse strings of the University of California and there was financial pressure on the academics to be seen to support his ideas. What the expert report actually said was: 'the association between self-esteem and its expected consequences is mixed, insignificant or absent.' (p209). But despite this, self-esteem prevails and hugely influences legislation and the outlook of Western society. The lie was up and running and no-one has stopped it yet.

The destructive implication

People are told, 'You are special'. But, since it is built on a lie, not only have social problems not been solved, nor have people become more fulfilled, but an enormously damaging corollary has been implied.

---

7   See – Frank Furedi, *Therapy Culture*, Routledge, 2004

It goes something like this: 'If I am really special, then all I need to be the person I want to be is within me'. (It's rather like Satan's lie in Genesis – you shall be as God). That might sound great, but hold on. 'If all I need is within me because I'm special, it must follow that it is actually my own fault if I am not what I would like to be'. Here we are – competitive souls, made according to Genesis to achieve – and if we fail to be what we want to be, we alone are responsible. There is no one to blame but ourselves.

Step back a moment once more. In our media-soaked world, what are young people told they should be? Who are the winners? It is those with the money, those with the success, those with the fame, those with the glamour (cf. 2 Tim. 3:1-5). The answer, of course, given the secular framework, is celebrities. They are the really significant people because everybody (the worldwide audience) knows them. But if I don't make it – I'm a loser. My life is worthless. And it is my own fault.

Social media

But then there's more. In the early twenty-first century, into the world of 'the special self' explodes digital technology. On top of the 'special self' is added 'the digital self,' with the advent of personal laptops, iPads and iPhones. Soon things like Facebook and Instagram become commonplace. Everyone is in touch with everyone. People begin to put online the perfect picture of themselves (a bit like saying – I'm so special I ought to be a celebrity). 'Here are all the cool things I do. How great is my life? Here are the photo-shopped pictures of myself from all the right angles. And, yes, I'm a bit like the air-brushed pictures of those gorgeous models and culture-shaping celebrities. In fact, I'm pretty nigh perfect, aren't I?'

But the problem is that deep down I know I'm not. I want to be (I was told by the culture I wanted to be). And it's all my fault because I believed it when they told me 'You're special' and that if I just believed in myself and tried my hardest, I could be anything I want to be. But I'm not! My life is not going where I meant it to go. I'm not in control of my life. I'm a loser.

And hence, the girls in particular begin to turn on themselves. And again, enhanced by some particular sequence of hurtful events in their lives and backed up by instantly knowing what the audience thinks – how many 'likes' they or 'dislikes' they have – and maybe exacerbated by online bullying – the competitive self turns on itself. Not only are the boys in trouble, the girls are in trouble too.

There may follow something like anorexia to somehow get back that feeling of control. There arises self-harming because of self-loathing because in her own estimate she's a loser. Self-harming can be seen as a cry for help, and crushed by the way they have been taught to see themselves and the world, many girls are in pain.

Recent research among 14-year-olds has indicated that 1 in 5 girls in Britain are self-harming. Self-harming among girls in the UK has risen 68% in three years.[8] And what is so interesting about this is that the iPhone was launched in 2007 just before research shows that happiness levels in girls started to decline. Made by God to compete, to achieve, this side of us has been subverted. For many, social media has become the forum for conflict and appears to be turning youngsters against themselves. This is in no way to blame the technology itself, but it's about the way the technology gets used in this current cultural climate of the self.

Atheism has produced an air-brushed celebrity/digital culture that leaves no way for many young people to be content with an ordinary life. 'There's just this life and I've blown it.' The teenaged

---

8   *The Week*, 8 September, 2018

years are years of vulnerability and self-doubt anyway as youngsters struggle to find their own identity and place in the world. But now has been added this new and very destructive way of thinking.

Back to the good news of Jesus

Of course, all this leads us back to the gospel of our Lord Jesus Christ. We have a generation of young men and women who are hurting and lost. Unlikely as it may seem in the present spiritual climate, they need to find their way back to God who made them. They must return to the God of the Bible, the living God who made them and in whom alone they can find forgiveness for self-obsession and fulfilment in life.

In Christ, we can embrace the worst about ourselves, because in his mysterious grace, God has sent his Son as a Saviour for real sinners. We can find our true identity as our life story becomes part of and coalesces with God's great adventure, his extraordinary love story of grace. We can fight 'the good fight' and find significance by achieving things for his kingdom, which may go unnoticed by this world, but are of eternal value.

This is what our contemporary world needs to hear.

Part Two:
Lovers Of Themselves

The sexual revolution and the church in current society

Introduction

The author Washington Irving, wrote the fanciful tale of a henpecked, work-shy man named *Rip Van Winkle*. Published in 1819, the story is set in late eighteenth-century America and tells how Rip lay down while squirrel hunting in the Catskill Mountains of New York State. Dulled by drink, he fell into a deep sleep. He awoke twenty years later, not realizing that he had slept more than a night.

There were signs something strange had occurred. His beard was a foot long, his dog was gone and his rifle was covered in rust. When he entered his village, he didn't recognize it. There were buildings he didn't remember. His clothes looked old fashioned. Children made fun of him. Rip proclaimed himself a loyal subject of King George III not realizing that while he had been asleep, the War of Independence had occurred and America was now its own country. He was out of place and he didn't know why.

Waking to a new reality

Many Christians today are having a similar experience. They may not have been physically asleep for twenty years, but they have maybe been cocooned in a little Christian bubble of Sunday church, Christian conferences, Christian books, Christian music, insulated against, and disconnected from, secular society. Now they are waking to the fact that the world has changed and things can't go on as they have before.

Whereas believers used to be thought somewhat odd but basically decent folk, now we are increasingly regarded as a harmful influence in society. We are now 'the bad guys'.[1] Whereas things like freedom of religion and freedom of speech were once regarded as absolute rights, such an outlook is now being challenged. You can lose your job for expressing certain ideas, especially biblical ideas concerning things like gender and marriage. Society is dramatically different – possibly in a way unprecedented in history. And it is likely to get worse before it gets better.

Pastors in a hurry

As an example of how much things have changed, Carl Trueman begins his landmark book on this subject by asking how the statement 'I am a woman trapped in a man's body' has come to look cogent and meaningful in today's society.[2] In the days of our grandfathers, such a statement would have been met with blank incredulity. But now it is taken very seriously indeed. What has happened?

Thankfully, some theologians and church leaders have begun to analyze things and to try to give a steer to the churches concerning the new situation we face. In my opinion, Carl Trueman's book *The Rise and Triumph of the Modern Self* is the most thorough and helpful introduction so far to our current situation. However, it is a big volume of over 400 pages of intensive thought and often closely argued reading for which many a busy pastor simply will not have time.

---

1   See Stephen MacAlpine, *Being the Bad Guys*, Good Book Company, 2021

2   Carl Trueman, *The Rise and Triumph of the Modern Self: Cultural Amnesia, Expressive Individualism, and the Road to the Sexual Revolution*, Crossway, 2020, page 19

So this part gives my own brief biblical introduction and then is mainly an attempt to sketch an overview of Trueman's work. My purpose is to get us thinking and hopefully for pastors to be able to give accessible teaching on the situation to God's people in the churches. After all, this is not simply a piece of fascinating contemporary history; it is something which may well cause faithful Christians to lose their friends and maybe their livelihoods.

1: Biblical background

Many cultural norms concerning sex and acceptable sexual behaviour have been swept away. In particular, the Christian view that mankind is composed of two genders, male and female (Gen. 1:27), and the Bible's teaching concerning marriage (Mt. 19:4-5), is in the process of being rejected as oppressive and damaging.

How have we got to this way of thinking? We need to get a grip on this firstly from Scripture. This seismic shift has not come out of nowhere, neither does it take the God of the Bible by surprise.

What happens when God is rejected?

For the last hundred years or more, secular thinkers have argued that God either doesn't exist or at least is an irrelevance to daily life. He could be dispensed with and very little would change. But the Bible says otherwise. To turn away from God affects a society at the deepest possible level. We should understand that this is the root of the titanic changes we are witnessing.

Here are three key NT passages which highlight what happens.

2 Timothy 3:1-4

> But mark this: There will be terrible times in the last days. People will be lovers of themselves, lovers of money, boastful, proud, abusive, disobedient to their parents, ungrateful, unholy, without love,

unforgiving, slanderous, without self-control, brutal, not lovers of the good, treacherous, rash, conceited, lovers of pleasure rather than lovers of God ...

Jesus taught that in the last days 'many will turn away from the faith' (Mt 24:10), rejecting God. Here Paul lists some of the bad fruit which must inevitably follow. But notice two things in particular. *First,* people become 'lovers of themselves'. The self is put above all else; hence Trueman's title, 'the rise of the modern self'. *Second,* that means, in practical terms, that people become 'lovers of pleasure rather than lovers of God'. Pleasure and personal 'feel good' are the priority. This is what loving yourself is about. And from the list of other sins Paul mentions consequent upon this, we can infer 'woe betide anyone who gets in the way'.

Ephesians 4:18-19

They [those without God] are darkened in their understanding and separated from the life of God because of the ignorance that is in them due to the hardening of their hearts. Having lost all sensitivity, they have given themselves over to sensuality so as to indulge in every kind of impurity, and they are full of greed.

These verses spell out the same trajectory towards hedonism for those who live without God. 'Having lost all sensitivity' to God and to spiritual things, they fill the void left in their hearts with sensuality. They 'give themselves over' to physical pleasures. And here Paul indicates that this heads in the direction of illicit sex, which will tend to extremes. This is where we are.

Romans 1:18-32

> The wrath of God is being revealed from heaven against all the godlessness and wickedness of people, who suppress the truth by their wickedness, since what may be known about God is plain to them, because God has made it plain to them. For since the creation of the world God's invisible qualities—his eternal power and divine nature—have been clearly seen, being understood from what has been made, so that people are without excuse.
>
> For although they knew God, they neither glorified him as God nor gave thanks to him, but their thinking became futile and their foolish hearts were darkened. Although they claimed to be wise, they became fools, and exchanged the glory of the immortal God for images made to look like mortal human being and birds and animals and reptiles.
>
> Therefore God gave them over in the sinful desires of their hearts to sexual impurity for the degrading of their bodies with one another ... God gave them over to shameful lusts. Even their women exchanged natural sexual relations for unnatural ones. In the same way the men also abandoned natural relations with women and were inflamed with lust for one another ... God gave them over to a depraved mind, so that they do what ought not to be done ...

In our third passage, note the parallel with the second. We have seen the apostle speaks of those who have 'given themselves over' to sensuality, but now we read that 'God gave them over' to their sinful desires and appetites as an expression of his wrath for their denial of him. When God is denied, society does not stay the same. It tends to become highly sexualized and aggressively so.

This is our society, our current culture. In some ways, Trueman's book simply traces in modern history the trajectory indicated by these Scripture texts. The Western world which used to be thought of as 'Christendom', has now become dominated by sex and sexual politics. While, down the years, there have always been libertines, it is now their ideas which command the culture. This societal move has taken centuries to emerge because a Christian morality and view of family has been the fundamental building block of Western society. But now that is being overthrown.

So, in this book, we will try to summarize Trueman's work as to how this has happened and is happening and note some of his conclusions.

Preliminaries

Before we get into the argument, there are some preliminary ideas which Trueman has borrowed from other modern thinkers and to which he refers.

Mimesis and Poiesis

> Put simply, these terms refer to two different ways of thinking about the world. A mimetic view regards the world as having a given order and meaning and thus sees human beings as required to discover that meaning and conform themselves to it. Poiesis, by way of contrast, sees the world as so much raw material out of which (our own) meaning and purpose can be created by the individual.[3]

It is clear that suppressing the truth of the Creator God and opting for no God invites us to Poiesis. We make of the world what we want with no-one to tell us what to do. And, of course, the astonishing advances in various technologies make this seem more credible. At one level, through surgery and chemicals, a man can become a woman if he/she wants to.

---

3 Trueman, page 39 – brackets my own

As Christians with an understanding of sin and the built-in rebelliousness of fallen human nature (Rom. 6:23), we can see that people would naturally prefer Poiesis to Mimesis. Many today see the world in Poiesis terms. 'You can be whatever you want to be.'

Three types of world

The American sociologist Phillip Reiff has a related idea. He spoke in terms of three types of worlds.

First worlds are pagan, with moral codes based on myths generally accepted by the society. Second worlds are those based on a faith in their God. Both first and second worlds, therefore, have a moral outlook founded in something transcendent, outside of people and this is a source of stability for those societies. Third worlds, by way of stark contrast, do not root their moral imperatives in anything sacred. There is nothing and no-one above themselves. They justify themselves and their actions on the basis of themselves. Rejecting God moves us into what Reiff would call a third world.

In fact, Reiff labels this kind of third world an 'anti-culture' because it sees the civilization and moral frameworks of first and second worlds as oppressive and restrictive of personal freedom. Thus, a third world deliberately attempts to destabilize and destroy first and second world cultural norms through what Reiff calls 'deathworks'. These are things which cynically make the old values look impotent and ridiculous. This is a primary aspect, for example, of pornography. Not only does it promote lust and treat people as mere 'things', but it repudiates any notion that sex has any significance beyond the pleasure of the act itself. Sex is simply fun and good, and those who want to restrict our desires, are prudish kill-joys.

In Reiffan terms, we now live in a third world, or at least on the brink of it.

2: The modern self and identity

Dispensing with God has reshaped how people now think of themselves and of others. Trueman writes:

> The underlying argument is that the sexual revolution, and its various manifestations in modern society, cannot be treated in isolation but rather must be interpreted as the specific and perhaps most obvious social manifestation of a much deeper and wider revolution in the understanding of what it means to be a self.[4]

Trajectory of the self

Here are the labels which we will use to summarize how Trueman sees the historical pathway of the self. These will enlighten us as to how we got to where we are now.

The 'psychological self' was followed by the 'romantic self'. This was succeeded by the 'plastic (or malleable) self'. Next came the explicitly 'sexual self', which has now, under the arguments of the New Left, become the 'sexually politicized self'. (I am paraphrasing here.)

All these are quite different from what we might propose as a biblical view of self, made in the image of God (Gen. 1:27), fallen but redeemed for Christ and to become like Christ. This might find

---

4 Trueman, page 35

reflection in the apostle Paul's famous words, describing himself as a sinner saved by grace, 'I have been crucified with Christ and I no longer live, but Christ lives in me. The life I now live in the body, I live by faith in the Son of God, who loved me and gave himself for me' (Gal. 2:20).[5] The Christian view of the self is very much an outward looking self. We look to God and to Christ for our salvation, meaning and identity. But the modern self is one that has turned inward on itself.

The psychological self

Our first stop en route as we come away from Reformation thinking into the period of the Enlightenment of the eighteenth century is with Jean-Jacques Rousseau (1712-1778). For Rousseau, people are intrinsically good until they are corrupted by the forces of society. (This of course, is very different from a Christian point of view). But he is the thinker who, instead of looking outward to God, invites the self to turn inward. The real identity of an individual is to be found in the inner psychological autobiography. Rousseau wrote of his *Confessions*: 'It is the history of my soul that I promised, and to relate it faithfully I require no other memorandum; all I need do, as I have done up until now, is to look inside myself.'[6]

Along with this went an emphasis on self-love, empathy and sympathy as the main informers of conscience and the tension between the individual and corrupt society.[7] Trueman comments

---

5 Will Storr has attempted a secular history of the self in his book *Selfie: How the West became self-obsessed*, Picador, 2018. In a rather distorted understanding of Scripture, he labels the Christian view of the self as 'The bad self'. His whole historical trajectory is as follows: The dying self; the tribal self; the perfectible self; the bad self; the good self; the special self; the digital self.

6 Trueman, page 129

7 Compare 2 Timothy 3:2

that in Rousseau 'we can see emerging the basic outlines of modern expressive individualism'.[8]

The romantic self

The poets of the late eighteenth and early nineteenth centuries, Wordsworth, Blake and Shelley, take the ideas of Rousseau from the intellectual elite and popularize them into mainstream culture. Rousseau's idea of society corrupting and brutalizing the innocent individual, seemed writ large in the days of the Industrial Revolution. The solution was to turn inward and back to an idealized rural existence.

Trueman states, 'Both Wordsworth and Shelley articulate views of poetry that press a clear connection between poetic aesthetics and ethics'.[9] True morality for these romantics was about what felt right and looked right to the individual. Once you look away from external frames of reference all 'moral' judgments tend to become nothing but expressions of personal preference or feeling. We enter a 'therapy culture'. This has major implications for sexual ethics. Authenticity as a human being is about being unashamed of one's own desires and acting on them.[10] Obviously, such thinking provides undergirding for both gay and lesbian agendas besides much else.

The plastic self

Plastic man is not simply psychological. He is, in Trueman's words, 'a man who thinks he can make and remake a personal identity at will'.[11]

---

8 Trueman, page 129
9 Trueman, page 142
10 Contrast Matthew 5:27-30; Romans 8:13
11 Trueman page 164

The foundations for such thinking were laid by the philosophers Frederich Nietzsche (1844-1900) and Karl Marx (1818-1883), and by the scientist Charles Darwin (1809-1882). Nietzsche is famous for his grim atheism which saw life as a power struggle and invites us to rise above human nature and become Übermench (overman). Marx saw industrial production and capitalism as not only changing society but reshaping people themselves and how they related to one another. Human nature is therefore plastic or malleable. Human nature is reduced from being a 'given' to being a product of the times, an historical phenomenon. It is not fixed.

Darwin's account of human origins reinforced this. People must accept that they are mere accidents of evolution and therefore not made in order to fulfil any kind of destiny. Darwin blurred the lines between the human and the animal and removed any idea of humanity having special status. We are ever evolving. We are a plastic species.

The sexual self

Sigmund Freud (1856-1939), the father of psychoanalysis, is a key figure in this story. He equated happiness with 'genital pleasure'. This is the point at which personal identity became equated with sex and sexuality. Now that idea dominates the Western world with people categorized according to their sexual desires: gay, bi, straight. For many, this is the most prominent truth about who you are.

If for Rousseau the natural man was innocent, for Freud the subconscious of human beings is dark, violent and irrational. For Freud, the job of the psychoanalyst was to excavate the unseen forces that live within us and bring them to the surface of consciousness. It is interesting that the inspiration for psychoanalysis was classical mythology (the Oedipus complex etc.).[12] In his book *Selfie*, Will Storr cites an expert as saying 'without the myths of ancient Greece ... there would be no psychoanalysis'.[13]

Freud places the sex drive at the very core of what it is to be human.[14] Before Freud sex was for procreation and pleasure (Prov. 5:19), – now it is who we really are. The happiest person is the one who is able to constantly indulge his or her sexual desires. However, this plays into the hands of powerful individuals, so we need civilization to curb this. So from a Freudian perspective, according to Trueman, 'it means that it is impossible for the civilized to be truly happy'.[15]

The sexually politicized self

Freud's ideas were later used to change the classic understanding of oppression. This is another crucial move in the story.

Because identity is about our inner self, especially our sexual desires, then victimhood becomes psychologized. The idea that oppression is about poverty or physical mistreatment is eclipsed. It is, in this case, those who feel unable to express their sexual desires, or whose sexual desires are deemed unacceptable by society, who are the oppressed. Oppression is about emotions.

Sex is no longer a private activity because it relates to our social identity. To outlaw or merely tolerate gay sex, for example, is to outlaw or merely tolerate a certain identity. It hits at the very heart of who a person believes themselves to be.

---

12 2 Timothy 4:4
13 Storr, page 113
14 It should be noted that if sex is at the centre of what it is to be human then children have to be sexualized. This is where the agenda for sex education to be pushed earlier and earlier comes from.
15 Trueman, page 164

Many university humanities departments have adopted so-called 'Critical Theory' and have latched on to this new angle on victimhood and oppression.[16] The New Left interprets traditional sexual codes as a malign strategy for maintaining the status quo in society. Western ideals must therefore be overthrown. The family is the authoritarian state in miniature. Dismantling the family is now, therefore, thought by many to be essential for political liberation. Sexual revolution is the way to achieve this. And this agenda is pushed even further by the philosopher Herbert Marcuse (1898-1979). Values such as tolerance are a sham, and simply a way of pacifying people to accept the patriarchal, capitalist power structure. The fight must be against educational institutions which teach tolerance. The New Left and it alone is equipped to see through the false claims of Western liberal democracy and consumerism and sexual freedom can be used to destabilize and bring them down.

Identity and community

Desire for inner happiness and psychological well-being lie at the heart of the modern era. This can be seen in the language of 2 Timothy 3 in terms of people becoming lovers of themselves. It is all about feeling good about yourself and making others feel good where possible.

As we have seen, it is now accepted that the way you see yourself, your inner image of yourself, is the true you. This even

---

16 Trueman summarizes the basic tenets of Critical Theory as follows: 1. The world can be divided between those who have power and those who do not; 2. The dominant Western narrative is really an ideological construct to preserve its own power structure; 3. The goal of Critical Theory is therefore to destabilize this power structure by destabilizing its dominant narratives that are used to justify it. (This includes things like natural gender, family and church - JB).

takes precedence over one's body.[17] This opens up the possibility of a difference between your biological sex and your gender. It is who you think you are that is your real identity regardless of whether you have XX or XY chromosomes. Hence the statement, 'I am a woman trapped in a man's body', now makes sense.

However, for one's identity to flourish it needs acknowledgement by others. The technical term is that identity is dialogical, i.e. it relies on language which is only developed through interaction with others. We are relational beings. We need the acceptance of other people in order to be comfortable with ourselves.

This means that society must serve the purpose of meeting the psychological needs of the individual. This is therapy culture. All institutions and communities (including the church) must adapt to reflect a therapeutic and inclusive mentality. Trueman tells us:

> The refusal by any individual to recognize an identity that society at large recognizes as legitimate is a moral offence, not simply a matter of indifference. The question of identity in the modern world is a question of dignity. For this reason, the various court cases in America concerning the provision of cakes and flowers for gay weddings are not ultimately about the flowers or the cakes. They are about the recognition of gay identity and, according to the members of the LGBTQ+ community, the recognition that they need in order to feel that they are equal members of society.[18]

This explains why the faithful church, upholding biblical teaching on gender, sexual intercourse exclusively within marriage between a man and woman, and the goodness of the traditional family is unlikely to be simply ignored. The Bible draws lines where current secular

---

17   This means that theologically the modern outlook can be classed as a form of Gnosticism.

18   Trueman, page 315.

ideology wants no lines. As with so many other things in which we all fail, same-sex attraction and the confusion of gender does not fit with God's good creation and therefore, in the long run, will not cause individuals or society to flourish. We face trouble.

3: Eroticism, the therapeutic and transgender

Sex and sexuality now dominate the Western world.

In his book, Trueman next highlights three 'triumphs'. These explore *first* how the erotic is pervasive in modern life; *second* how especially crucial legal decisions are now made on the basis of emotivism and aesthetics; and *third*, how transgenderism has made headway in society.

Eroticism

The sexual revolution has meant that, from TV soap operas to teenaged pop music, our culture is now saturated with sexual themes.

The prevalence of pornography is especially noteworthy. Here, of course, technology has played a part. If freedom and happiness are encapsulated in sexual satisfaction, then online pornography becomes the obvious, the easiest and the most private (it seems) medium of liberation and fulfilment.

Pornography epitomizes the sexual revolution because it presents sex as merely recreational – a physical, pleasurable act that is divorced from any greater relational significance or transcendence. It detaches sex from any ethical context.[19]

And attitudes have changed. Pornography is no longer seen as an example of male dominance and violence against women. There is even talk of 'ethically sourced' pornography – that is where women are not in any way coerced to participate and the 'rights of performers' are respected. Trueman says:

> The philosophical claim I am making here is that the normalization of pornography in mainstream culture is deeply connected to the mainstream culture's rejection of sacred order. Pornography carries with it a philosophy of sex and of what it means to be human that is inimical to traditional religious perspectives, in the West's case primarily Christianity. It is therefore both symptomatic and constitutive of the de-created, desacralized world that emerges in modern times, with roots in Rousseau and Romanticism, and given sharp expression in philosophical and scientific idioms by Marx, Nietzsche, Darwin, Freud and the New Left. The triumph of pornography is both evidence of the death of God and one of the means by which he is killed.[20]

It is a 'deathwork'. Some sociological research shows there is a clear link between pornography use and the rejection of traditional religious belief particularly among teenagers.

The therapeutic

Earlier in his *opus*, Trueman referred to the philosopher Alasdair MacIntyre and his book *After Virtue* which argues that modern moral theories are incapable of explaining the rational authority of moral

---

19   This is the impression given, even though pornography is often related to depression, suicide and sex-trafficking.

20   Trueman, page 297

norms. Into this void left by the failure of modern ethical theory has stepped what MacIntyre termed 'emotivism' – in which all evaluative judgments/moral judgments are 'nothing but expressions of preference of attitude or feeling'.

Here we are back with emotions and aesthetics being the main informers of conscience, as advised by the Romantic poets. This is where morality and ethics ends up in 'the last days' described in 2 Timothy 3, where people are lovers of themselves and lovers of pleasure rather than lovers of God. 'Essentially emotivism presents preferences as if they were truth claims'.[21] This is therapy culture in the courtroom.

As we saw earlier, all of a society's institutions must adapt to promote the psychological well-being of the individual. This has now entered the realm of the judiciary.

Commenting of the case of *Obergefell v. Hodges* from which the Supreme Court legalized gay marriage in the USA, Trueman says that the ethical logic used was mere emotivism consonant with the attitudes of sexualized therapeutic culture. He writes concerning the judgment:

> It is emotivism. Those parts of tradition that support contemporary tastes are proof positive of the correctness of the opinion; those that are not useful in supporting the desired conclusion or that stand in opposition to contemporary tastes can be dismissed as outmoded or motivated by bigotry or simply ignored. And the court can safely do this because it is speaking to a society at large that thinks precisely the same way. The ruling and its supporting arguments are absolutely connected to, and dependent on, the changes in thinking about selfhood, human

---

21   Trueman, page 85

nature, sexuality, and the nature of oppression and liberty that we have traced ... earlier.[22]

Transgender

We have seen that identity is now seen in terms of a self which is psychologized, sexual and able to create or recreate itself. This paves the way for the idea of a person who sees themselves as being of one gender trapped inside a body of another gender, (or indeed no longer wishing to be categorized as either male or female). Such ideas are seen as coherent in a society which places a decisive priority on the psychological over the physical in determining identity.

The LGBTQ+ coalition stands together against the traditional sexual norms of society. Transgender people make common cause with lesbians, gay men and bisexual people because they perceive heterosexual normativity as the common enemy.

However, the coalition does not easily fit together. There are contradictions within it. Both gay men and lesbians, speak of themselves as being same-sex attracted. But that presupposes there are fixed genders. Those who argue for transgender and beyond do not accept the idea of fixed genders. They see gender on a spectrum and also as a fluid concept.

The status of transwomen (men who have become women) is a cause of acrimonious dispute among those older feminists who campaigned for women's rights. The classic feminists feel that the whole status of being a woman is undermined and depoliticized by transgenderism. Many feel that you cannot dissociate the female from female history and from the experience of what it is to grow

---

22   Trueman, page 315

up as a female physically. But 'being a woman is now something that can be produced by a technique – literally prescribed by a doctor'.[23]

Transgenderism seems to repudiate the significance of the body for selfhood (in line with the way the self has been psychologized) and this means a repudiation of parents, the ones who conceived, gave birth to and brought up the little girl or boy. Trueman quotes Germaine Greer: 'Whatever else it is, gender reassignment is an exorcism of the mother'.[24]

Transgender is a radical mentality which says, 'my identity is entirely of my own making'. Given the tacit atheism of Western society this is of course Poiesis rather than Mimesis.

---

23 Trueman, page 360
24 Trueman, page 375

4: What to think through

As we come to terms with this description of the sexual revolution and the world in which we now live, we ought to recognize that not everything about that is going on is bad. There are two things in particular which Christians would do well to note.

The first is dignity.

'With Rousseau's emphasis on the individual and the state of nature as the ideal, the shift to individual, intrinsic dignity is clear. And that is something with which the Christian should sympathize. We are not supposed to regard the life of a poor person as of any less value than that of a wealthy or important public figure'.[25] But today this dignity is detached from any sacred order. It is not rooted in all people being made in God's image (Jas. 3:9).

The second is authenticity.

Though Trueman doesn't say this, the concern of the sexual revolution for people to be outwardly what they are inwardly, does find a positive echo in the NT – not in a sinful way but in a godly way. A great theme of Jesus' Sermon on the Mount is authenticity – that religious acts must come from the heart, and not be a sham (Mt 5:27–28; 6:1). We can recognize a right concern for honesty about oneself

---

25   Trueman, page 387

instead of hypocrisy. True conversion is about the inner heart being right, not just the outward actions.

But having said those things, there are other areas where Christians need to be extremely wary and discerning.

Engaging with LGBTQ+ issues

Much of what is involved in the sexual revolution the Bible calls sinful and perverted (Rom. 1:26–27). However, the issues are related not just to sex but to identity.

In particular, the Christian needs to beware of simply adopting the world's stance when thinking about and discussing these issues. Is the church meant to look 'plausible' to the world in its teaching about sexual ethics? If Scripture is right (as we believe it is) that the sexual revolution originates in a denial of God, how can that possibly be? How can the 'God logic', that humanity's highest happiness is found in Christ and that all else in our lives should be subservient to that, be made plausible in terms of 'anti-God logic'? It is an attempt to square the circle. Our job here is to love all people and remain faithful.

We can easily slip into using the categories of the world which are misleading and militate against clarity on key issues. The idea that our true identity is sexual is a category mistake. The Genesis account tells us that sex is a function of who we are (Gen. 1:28), not who we are (Gen. 1:27). The world's thinking here confuses ontology with something of teleology. Adam was a true human being before he ever had sex with Eve.

If the world's categories, represented by the acronym LGBTQ+, rest on a basic category mistake (that sexual desire is identity) should not the Christian critique this rather than simply engage with it or allow themselves to be defined within this framework? To concede the categories can be to concede the argument.

Trueman writes: 'The framework for identity in wider society is deep rooted, powerful and fundamentally antithetical to the kind of identity promoted as basic in the Bible'.[26]

Sexual morality

The sexual revolution has been built on the idea that sex is meant to simply be recreational fun. The consequences of 'free love' have been handled/avoided through abortion and medicine. But deep diffculties have begun to emerge.

First, the 'free love' approach, as Freud foresaw, favours the powerful.

This means men generally, but particularly there have been abuse scandals in which women and girls have been abused by rich and influential men. The #MeToo movement has rightly exposed this. The world recognizes the horror of these things.

Second, under the sexual revolution, sex is meant to be fine between 'consenting adults'.

But as many court cases have found, defining consent is very diffcult. What one partner took to be consent was not meant like that by the other partner. All this, even on its own terms, cries out for setting sex within a moral framework. But, of course, this is the last thing the sexual revolution wants to see. This will not serve, for example, the New Left's agenda of using sex to destabilize traditional Western norms.

---

26   Trueman, page 393

Gay marriage

The book *After the Ball: How America Will Conquer Its Fear And Hatred of Gays*, by neuropsychologist Marshall Kirk and advertising executive Hunter Madsen, was published in 1989, and it advised the gay community that if it wanted to gain acceptance it needed to project a more cute and cuddly image of itself. Gay marriage has now arrived and has all the right therapeutic rhetoric and images on its side. It seems as if it is here to stay and faithful Christians will need to think through how to cope and address this fact.

It may be that its weakness will be the way that marriage has had to be redefined in order to make room for it. Perhaps the door has been opened by the legislation to other forms of 'marriage' which will not prove so appealing to the Western public. For example, does it make polygamous arrangements possible, which may well lead to the misuse and abuse of women?

When we mix same-sex marriage with transgenderism more problems arise. Trueman tells the story of a lesbian marriage in which one of the women changed sex to become a man. The partner was left in total confusion mentally. She now didn't know who she was. Was she a 'straight' wife married to a man? Or if she was a lesbian, why was she with a man in marriage?

Religious freedom

The United Nations, in paragraph 18 of its Universal Declaration of Human Rights, guarantees freedom of religion and freedom to change religion. But the expressive individualism of the sexual revolution is putting pressure on religious freedom.

The general decline in religious commitment in the West, and especially the loss of younger people from the churches, means that society doesn't care very much about religious freedom.

Religious people and Christians are vulnerable to having their freedoms curtailed if not removed. In the West, it is presently thought that sexual desire is the key to personal identity and therefore the dignity of every individual. This trumps religious freedom. Religious restrictions on sexual activity are seen as oppressive. This means that society sees the church as something it would probably be better off without.

The church is seen as an overwhelmingly white and middle-class institution and this does not help.

5: Responding as churches?

How are the churches to begin to respond to the situation in which they now find themselves? Some conservative evangelicals have simply continued their same old path hoping that the things we have discussed will simply go away or pass them by. That is unlikely to happen. Other churches have compromised on the Bible's clear teaching on sexual ethics or at least tried to create some 'wiggle room' for people to identify as 'gay Christians' for example.

Every pastor needs to open his Bible with humility and prayer as to how to best lead the church at this time. Here are three suggestions as to what we need to concentrate on.

Biblical identity

If Trueman is correct in seeing that the sexual revolution has been driven by a false understanding of the human self, then surely one of the first things that conservative evangelical churches ought to be doing is giving clear Bible teaching concerning human identity.

This will involve clear and convincing teaching which opposes atheistic evolution and underlines that humanity's true identity lies in the high calling of being made in God's image. We were made in the image of God and, fallen as we now are, redemption in Christ includes our taking off the old self and putting on the new self, 'which is being renewed in knowledge in the image of its Creator' (Col. 3:9-10). Among other things this will include teaching on what it is to be the image of God, what it is to be fallen, what it is to be redeemed. Teaching on having a high view of the physical body will be important along with such things as a biblical understanding of work, art, sexuality, ethnicity, justice etc.[27]

Explicitly, when a young man comes to his pastor and says 'I think I'm gay' or a girl goes privately to her mother and confesses 'I think I might be a lesbian', along with love, the first response needs to be something like 'but you are so much more than your current sexual temptations'. The contemporary world narrows people down to their hormones – especially on social media. But human beings are gloriously so much bigger than mere sex machines. The whole history of mankind's achievements in science, art and humanitarianism shouts this from the rooftops. We are God's offspring (Acts 17:28). And pastor, our sermons must be such as to facilitate a prison breakout from the ugly solitary confinement of trivialized sensual humanity. Humanity is being trashed and we are called to rescue it.

Right and wrong

As we have seen, when people are lovers of themselves then what is good tends to be seen as what 'feels good' and bad what makes us 'feel bad'. And the church easily gets sucked into this way of thinking, because making people immediately feel better seems so loving – and love is indeed a Christian virtue.

But even common sense tells us that this is too simplistic. Chemotherapy for cancer does not make a sufferer feel good, but terribly bad, at least to begin with – but it is what they need if they are going to be cured. In spiritual terms, conviction of sin is not a

---

27 See for example Owen Strachan, *Re-enchanting Humanity: a theology of mankind*, Mentor Christian Focus, 2019

nice feeling, but it does lead us to see our need of Christ and his cross and brings us to salvation (Acts 2:37). Trueman writes:

> The church should reflect long and hard on the connection between aesthetics and her core beliefs and practices. I noted above that one of the hallmarks of ethical discussion today is its dependence on personal narratives ... personal narratives (are) presented as incontrovertible precisely because they are personal testimonies – the highest form of authority in an age of expressive individualism. And this aesthetic concern reflects the perennial power of sympathy and empathy in shaping morality ... The church needs to respond to this aesthetic-based logic, but first of all she needs to be consciously aware of it. And that means that she herself must forgo indulging in, and thereby legitimating, the kind of aesthetic strategy in the wider culture. The debate on LGBTQ+ issues within the church must be decided on the basis of moral principles, not the attractiveness and appeal of the narratives involved ... That is not to say that pastoral strategies aimed at individuals should not be compassionate, but what is and what is not compassionate must always rest on deeper, transcendent principles.[28]

This really amounts to a call to the churches to come back to the Bible and its truths. Christianity is to be in the proper sense doctrinal and dogmatic.

Church as family

As we have already seen, human selfhood depends on community. Our identity is at least partially constructed by our social interactions with others. We find ourselves amidst the sum total of our relationships and our social environment.

---

28 Trueman, pages 402-403

This means that if the church is to help people find and maintain their true identity, then churches must be communities which mirror and build the image of God in people. A church should not be cultish. It should be a home for true humanity. It should be a family. And there should be a deep humility, recognizing that every saint has a past and every sinner has a future, under Christ's kingship.

Churches which have chosen to operate as corporations or educational institutions, really miss the point of what the NT churches were like. The phrase 'brothers and sisters' really meant something. As the world misleads people about their true identity, this aspect of church will become increasingly crucial.

Part Three:
Soft Totalitarianism

A wake-up call to churches and Christian leaders

Introduction

God's people are to watch and be alert to their times, especially when those times pose a threat to the gospel and the church (Mk 13:37).

Totalitarianism is back on the agenda. We thought that, following the end of the Cold War, it was consigned to the dustbin of history. But it is threatening a comeback – in a different form.

Totalitarianism is not so much about domination by a particular individual (dictatorship) but the absolute rule of an approved ideology which brooks no discussion and punishes any dissent. It is a form of government which intentionally sets out to eradicate all previous traditions, outlooks and ideas (like Christian teaching) and replace them with its own way of thinking with the aim of bringing every facet of life under its control.

Climate of fear

When we hear the word 'totalitarianism' we might think of jackboots, secret police and labour camps as in Stalin's USSR or Nazi Germany. But a new form seems to be emerging in the Western world of the twenty-first century – the place where we live now. It has been called 'soft totalitarianism'.[1] It is being promoted not so much by any particular political party or national government but by the emerging culture around us. It has infiltrated politics, business corporations

---

1   See for example Rod Dreher, *Live Not By Lies*, Sentinel, 2020

and the media and has begun to change the laws of the land in the name of 'progress'.

Already we find, just as behind the old 'Iron Curtain', we must be careful what we say in public and what thoughts we let slip in an email or text message. There are no secret informers or police raids in the dead of night, nevertheless information on us all is available and monitored via digital technology. Saying what is deemed the wrong thing (what is currently politically incorrect) can bring unprecedented abuse and calls for punishment on social media, with devastating consequences. Free speech is under attack and a climate of fear is being generated.

The church, like the men of Issachar, must understand the times if we are to know what to do (1 Chr. 12:32). We must recognize that this new form of totalitarianism, which seems on the verge of taking over, is just as atheistic and as determined to annihilate the faithful church and Christian values as any twentieth century Communist or Fascist regime.

This part is an attempt to give a basic understanding of what has been happening, what may well happen and to sound a wake-up call to the churches.

An anatomy of totalitarianism

Historically, totalitarian regimes, whether of the Right or Left politically, displayed three common elements.[2]

- The first is a 'Promised Land' vision of the idealized future which is guaranteed by the totalitarian ideology. The whole forward thrust of society, it is said, must be directed to this

---

2 See for example Christopher Booker in *The Seventies*, published by Allen Lane, 1980, page 72

end. This defines progress. We might call this the 'eschatology' of the movement

- The second is a fanatical loyalty to the cause based on the perceived 'rightness' of the ideology. For twentieth century totalitarianism, this loyalty was focused on the leaders of the movement who were treated like demigods. One thinks of the giant wall posters of Lenin, Stalin or Mao. These were the 'prophets' – the all-seeing 'Big Brothers' of the movement – to whom unquestioning obedience was due
- The third is the identification of 'the enemy', the psychic personification of something to struggle against. For the Nazis, it was sadly the Jews. For the Communists, it was Western capitalism and the bourgeoisie. The movement must have a 'demonology'.

This is the basic anatomy of totalitarian systems. There are of course, large differences between twentieth century totalitarian regimes and the imminent cultural totalitarianism of the twenty-first century. However, this basic analysis will serve as a worthwhile guide to what is going on today.

1: Social justice?

Christians ought to be much in favour of social justice (Amos 5:24). We are called to 'act justly, and to love mercy and to walk humbly with [our] God' (Mich. 6:8).

But today's 'Social Justice' – indicated by capital letters – is very different from the biblical view of justice. Originating in Left-wing university Humanities departments, it is a movement that has sadly taken a hugely sinister turn in recent years. We may well be facing the rise of 'one of the least tolerant and most authoritarian ideologies that the world has ever had to deal with.'[3]

The promise of the movement is equality. In many ways this is a fine vision. But notice that it is different from the aim of the classic liberal outlook of the Western world, which was personal freedom. Actually, secular ideas of freedom and equality turn out to be a zero-sum game. As we will see, maximizing one requires restricting the other.

How should we understand the Social Justice movement? Here is a brief overview in five steps.

---

3   Helen Pluckrose and James Lindsay, *Cynical Theories: how universities made everything about race, gender and identity – and why this harms everybody*, Swift Publishing, 2020, page13.

Step One: Secularism

Exclusion of God – the real God who has made himself known through Jesus, his living word (Jn. 1:1,14), and the Bible, his written word (2 Tim. 3:16) – is foundational to the whole of the Social Justice project. Humanity takes centre stage. God and his laws have no place. This is the stable from which this movement comes.

As Christians, that must alert us immediately to problems. Scripture assures us that 'the fool says in his heart "There is no God"' (Ps. 14:1). Paul the apostle writes of those who reject God, 'Although they claimed to be wise, they became fools' (Rom. 1:22).

Step two: Postmodernism

Without God there is no ultimate frame of reference outside of ourselves to determine what is right and true. The secular modernism of the Enlightenment imagined that human reason and science on their own, could establish truth and would produce an equal and just society in which people would be free and fulfilled. But that has not happened. And so this optimistic vision of modernism is now seen as a failure and has given way to post-modernism (PM).

- *First*, PM rejects any absolute truth and adopts a through-going relativism (Judg. 21:25). Reason alone cannot establish truth. Reason is a process which will lead in different directions depending on one's starting assumptions
- *Second*, with this mindset, PM sees reality as incoherent and fragmented. It specifically rejects any overarching explanation of our world (metanarrative) whether it is that of science, Marxism or Christianity

- *Third*, because there is no common truth on which to build, language becomes a mere system of signs with the meaning intended by an author or speaker impossible to know
- *Fourth*, all claims to truth on the part of various groups or individuals are seen simply as power-plays designed to manipulate other people. All interaction between people is not really about communication but about power.

It is very negative. Because all truth claims are not true and are manipulative, they must be debunked. This will save you from falling into the clutches of those who pretend to have the truth. Disbelief is the only safe choice. This is the very opposite to the classical approach of 'keeping an open mind'. All claims to truth must be 'deconstructed' – critiqued, problematized and disparaged.

Step three: Anti-normality

Many situations in the world are genuinely unfair and should be rectified through compassionate action founded on reason and, where necessary, the democratic process.

But Social Justice rejects this approach to injustice and insists on a radically different line. With its aim of equality and including every group of people on an absolutely even footing, Social Justice deploys the postmodern approach of deconstructionism to undermine and attack any idea of what is 'normal'.

Anything accepted as normal in society would inevitably disadvantage any group which does not fall into that category. So norms and the category of 'normal' itself, especially as they pertain to society, must be trashed. This alone will make everyone the same.

Any idea that the majority of people have chosen what is normal because it works best given the way reality is, must be thrown out.

Given such 'critical theory', even identifying people's straightforward physical appearance – like male and female, hairy and bald men, black and white people, able-bodied and disabled – has become a major problem. Such categories cannot be seen as 'givens'. Instead, they are said to be offensive and culturally constructed by 'normal' society to protect itself; to keep its privilege and power. Humans are not born male or female but have a gender assigned to them by the biased expectations of 'normalcy'. For example, simply speaking, a 'man' is only male because his parents and normal society told him he is. Social Justice's more extreme adherents see science as a construct of White Anglo-Saxon Male culture and say its findings should not be taken as a valid for everyone.[4]

Step four: Double-think

However, although the post-modern basis for Social Justice denies the existence of universal truth or any reliable engagement with reality through language, at this point some 'double think' is introduced. With absolute equality as its sole concern, the only 'given' allowed in Social Justice thinking is the truth and reality of suffering and oppression. The pain of the disadvantaged is real (which of course it is). This gives Social Justice theory a foothold in the real world and empowers it to argue and accuse. Suddenly language becomes meaningful and important.

Though postmodernism proper would admit that it is not possible to know with certainty whether anyone's suffering is real or not, with this piece of double-think Social Justice ideology appears incontrovertible. Who could possibly argue that 'equality' is a bad aim? To reject 'justice' is, of course, to condemn oneself. And so, as

---

4   This 'anti-normalism' can be related to 'lawlessness' and the end-time 'man of lawlessness', 2 Thessalonians 2:3.

with other forms of totalitarianism, Social Justice seeks to eradicate all previously accepted ideas. 'Normality' must go.

Step five: Political Activism

Social Justice advocates set themselves up as judges of mankind. Through their activities, words like 'de-platforming' and 'cancel culture' have entered our dictionaries.

The underlying assumption, which is central to the Social Justice outlook, is that bigotry and injustice are everywhere (except in their movement). The job of the activist is to scrutinize every speech, text, event, supposed mindset and attitude with the purpose of exposing, denigrating and purging the public square of everything and everyone which does not match their ideas and is not 'politically correct'.[5] Thus, the climate of fear grows and the totalitarian ideology, which tolerates no dissent, is imposed.

Meanwhile 'because of its rejection of objective truth and reason, postmodernism (and therefore Social Justice) refuses to substantiate itself, and cannot, therefore, be argued with'.[6] In effect Social Justice has set itself up as the great, unchallengeable 'given' to which everyone and everything must bow the knee.

---

5 A phrase which I think I am correct in saying, first appears in the writings of Lenin.

6 See Pluckrose and Lindsay, *Cynical Theory*, page 38, (brackets mine).

2: Surveillance society

Conservative evangelical churches are on a collision course with the agenda of the Social Justice movement.

We believe in God the Creator (Gen. 1:1), who has given mankind freedom to live within the limits of various norms which he built into the world from the beginning. These things were written into the human conscience. But, according to Social Justice theory, norms for humanity are the root of inequality and therefore must be destroyed and conscience relegated to the status of just another cultural construct.

The Social Justice movement desires a revolution which will root out all the old ways of thinking and those who hold to them. Such people must be identified. Therefore, surveillance becomes a critical tool of this revolution.

Underground Christianity

During the days of the twentieth century totalitarian regimes, the churches had to go underground in an attempt to avoid drawing attention to themselves and subsequent persecution (Mt. 10:21-23).

This was not simply a strategy of the church. Writing of ordinary citizens in Stalin's USSR, Orlando Figes says: 'In a society where it was thought that people were arrested for loose tongues, families survived by keeping to themselves. They learned to live double lives, concealing from the eyes and ears of dangerous neighbours, and sometimes even from their own children, information and opinions, religious beliefs, family values and traditions ... that clashed with Soviet public norms'.[7] They were in fear of being found to have said something 'politically incorrect'.

The great difference between now and the twentieth century is the surveillance potential of today's digital technology and the internet. Thankfully, Social Justice advocates do not yet govern these powerful tools. But we need to be aware of the direction in which things are moving.

Big brother is watching

Companies like Google, Facebook and Amazon are inexorably moving towards knowing far too much about us.[8]

In 1998 Google became an incorporated company with a laudable mission to liberate information and make it available worldwide. But as people searched the web, they left their own digital fingerprints. For example, in addition to key words, each Google search query produces a wake of collateral data such as the number and pattern of search terms, how the query is phrased, spelling, punctuation, dwell times, click patterns and location. To begin with this extra information was stored but ignored. It was a young Stanford University graduate, Amit Patel, who it seems, first saw that using the statistical methods of behavioural science, this 'accidental' information could be put to use. He concluded that detailed stories about each user – thoughts, feelings, interests – could be constructed from the wake of every

7   Orlando Figes, *The Whisperers: private life in Stalin's Russia*, Penguin 2008, page xxxii

8   See for example, Shoshona Zuboff, *The Age of Surveillance Capitalism: the fight for a human future at the new frontier of power*, Profile Books, 2019

online transaction. This information could be sold to those selling products online. It helps to know your customers.

The future possibilities as the technology advances are frightening. Artificial intelligence can pick up on behaviours which elude the computer user's own mind. Given enough data it can predict how a person will react to different situations. This ability easily slides over into seeking to modify and even control an individual's belief and behaviour as the relevant personalized stimuli are placed on the screen before them.

This technology, reminiscent of the two-way screens in the home in George Orwell's classic dystopian novel *Nineteen Eighty-Four*, is something a totalitarian regime would love to get its hands on in order to monitor and control the population. The internet provides the makings of an all-seeing 'Big Brother' for the twenty-first century.

Many Christians and churches have bought into the new technology without giving it much thought. We assumed that convenience is a greater priority than privacy. But now is the time we must ask ourselves some questions.

Capitalism and influence

Despite promises of government safeguards, people's personal information is bought and sold between businesses. At present this information is generally used to market products which will commend themselves to targeted personalities. But there are signs that things are changing.

In his book, *Live Not By Lies*, Rod Dreher asks: 'Why should corporations and institutions not use the information they harvest to manufacture consent to some beliefs and ideologies and to manipulate the public into rejecting others?'[9] The idea would be, for example, 'you cannot use our online banking unless you sign up to our code of ethics.'

And pressure is being applied to companies to try to make sure this happens. If a company is seen not to sign up to Social Justice doctrines then it often faces a storm of social media protest from activists and withdrawal of endorsements from celebrities, which might well devastate the balance sheet. Consumer power and public image has vast influence. This is how the Social Justice movement is beginning to turn the screw and impose its totalitarian vision.

Further, the masters of the internet lean in the direction of Social Justice. The journalist and author, Douglas Murray, writes: 'As anybody who has spent any time there will know, the political atmosphere of Silicon Valley is several degrees to the left of a liberal arts college. Social justice is assumed to be ... the default setting for all employees in the major companies and most of them, including Google, put applicants through tests to weed out anyone with wrong ideological inclinations. Those who have gone through these tests recount that there are multiple questions on issues to do with diversity – sexual, racial and cultural – and that answering these questions 'correctly' is a prerequisite for getting a job'.[10]

Social Justice is on the road to becoming worldwide 'Google ethics.'

9   Rod Dreher, *Live Not By Lies: A manual for Christian dissidents*, Sentinel Books, 2020, page 79

10 *The Madness of Crowds: Gender, Race and Identity*, by Douglas Murray, Bloomsbury Continuum, 2019, page 110

3: Christians as the enemy

The three classic ingredients of totalitarianism we identified earlier are arguably emerging before our eyes in the Social Justice movement.

- *First*, there is a Utopian vision of the promised future to work towards. This is complete 'equality'.
- *Second*, there is fanatical loyalty to the values of the cause.[11] The Social Justice agenda is seen as unassailably 'right'.
- *Third*, there is the identification of 'the enemy' against which the movement must fight and seek to eliminate.

These three work together to provide the dynamic and momentum of totalitarianism.

Why totalitarianism needs enemies

Since Social Justice pursues 'anti-normalism' in the quest for equality, any group which believes in certain 'givens' or norms for society,

---

11 In the past this was channelled towards icons of the 'prophets' of the revolution – like Lenin or Marx. That has not appeared yet for 'soft totalitarianism' and perhaps never will. The dominant images of 'Big Brother' are too much associated with hard-line twentieth century totalitarian regimes and would be counterproductive. However, the endorsement of the Social Justice agenda by the eye-catching icons of 'celebrity' culture may well perform something of the same function.

become the foe. This includes religious people like traditional Jews, Muslims and Christians and also anyone, even secular people, who still operate within the framework of traditional categories, morality and outlook.

Totalitarianism must have an enemy. It is part of the glue that holds the movement together. It is necessary to the Social Justice cause that we, and people like us, be demonized. So faithful Christians and churches where the Bible and its values are taught should not be surprised if they are targeted, by Social Justice activists, with attempts to take us to court in coming days. It doesn't matter if you are kind to the poor or are poor yourself, if you do not sign up to the Social Justice agenda, you are the enemy.

George Orwell recognized why totalitarian regimes need an enemy. It gives the regime someone to blame for all the woes of the world and to use to divert attention away from themselves when their ideology fails to deliver. The thinking of the world is then to say 'It's all those repressive Christian ideas that are the trouble!' Further, in his novel *Nineteen Eighty-Four*, each citizen is required to join in the daily two minutes of hate in which, following a propaganda film depicting the evils of 'Emmanuel Goldstein', citizens should loudly and vehemently express their animosity and abhorrence of this enemy.[12] The hate session was a point of unity for the population.

One cannot but note the parallels which exist between Orwell's 'two minutes of hate' and the bullying, judgmentalism and hate that is currently expressed on social media against anyone who publicly fails to toe the 'party line' as required by Social Justice.

---

12   I am sure the connotations of the name 'Emmanuel' (Mt. 1:23) were not lost on Orwell.

Why faithful Christians are in the firing line

Think about it. We believe in God in a society that doesn't. We trust a God-given, inerrant Bible as teaching us the truth when the postmodernism which sustains Social Justice rejects universal truth and caricatures it as a power play. We believe all people (including ourselves) are sinners in need of salvation in a world which thinks that people are good enough as they are with no need to repent of anything. We preach Christ as the only way of salvation in a society which insists there are many ways to find 'God'. We believe that male and female are norms for humanity at a time when gender is increasingly accepted as fluid. We stand for male-female marriage when marriage has been redefined. We are pro-life in days when our culture has been subverted to become militantly pro-choice. We believe in male servant-headship in both family and the church, because that is what the Bible teaches, at a time when all authority is seen as oppressive. We believe that the natural family is the building block of society after years in which the norm of family life has been under constant attack. We believe that parents have the right and the responsibility to care and correct and decide on their children's education, when governments are arrogating that right for themselves. And we could add to that list. Therefore, faithful Christians and Bible-teaching churches must inevitably become targets for the 'soft totalitarianism' of Social Justice.

Church leaders and pastors should alert their congregations to what is happening and prepare them to be able to stand through the inevitable coming storm, whatever form that may take.

Persecution and propaganda

The attack on the churches is twofold. There is both threat and the siren voice of compromise. God's people have faced these things before.

In the days of Daniel, the three friends, Shadrach, Meshach and Abednego, were called to worship the golden image that presided over the multi-cultural, inclusive empire of Nebuchadnezzar's Babylon. Failure to do so would mean the fiery furnace (Dan. 3:6). But these brave men refused to worship anything other than the true God. 'If we are thrown into the blazing furnace, the God we serve is able to deliver us from it, and he will deliver us from our Majesty's hand. But even if he does not, we want you to know, Your Majesty, that we will not serve your gods or worship the image of gold you have set up' (Dan. 3:17-18). Today's Christians may not face a fiery furnace but just see what happens at your place of work if, for example, you fail to endorse 'rainbow' values or a gay pride march.

Pastors need to be teaching and standing alongside their people who face such threats.

But the ways of totalitarianism include not just the iron fist but the kid glove. There is much done through the secular media to gently sow doubts about biblical truth and values and to cause Christians to question whether they really need to take a clear stand.

The sexual inclusivism of many TV reports and situation comedies parade the idea of what might be called 'secular grace'. The message is that 'morals are relative, a matter of opinion, we are all aware of our own failures, so we just accept everyone – like grace'. It is almost as if this secular grace is more gracious than God's grace; it not only accepts people as they are, it doesn't try to change them. And even Christians can be left with the impression that by comparison the gospel looks narrow and the church too stiff and starchy.

What these things rarely show you is the damage done, especially to women and children, by the permissive society and the mental health problems it leaves in its wake. And, of course, secular grace is cheap. It costs very little for one imperfect person to cut another imperfect person some slack. But for an all-holy God to legitimately forgive sinners, it took the blood of Calvary (Rom. 3:25-26).

Pastor you need to teach and inoculate your people against the oncoming cultural climate.

4: Christianity and Common Sense

The Social Justice/Politically Correct agenda has serious repercussions for society. For one thing, even without the climate of fear and threats to dissenters, it leads to the death of logical thought.

Writing in *The Sunday Times* in 1999, the late Professor Roger Scruton foresaw this. He said: '"Deconstruction", "difference", "gender" – these are terms used to create an area of thought in the absence of thought, and turn out to mean next to nothing … The fact is that debate and rational argument no longer have a central place in the world of the young, and not only because the sound-bite culture has pushed them aside. Children are taught from an early age not to judge between opinions – to be 'sensitive' towards other cultures and other ways of thinking. If all options are equally valid, then none of them really matters – such is the inevitable conclusion of the multicultural and inclusive curriculum.'

Foolishness

In Professor Scruton's words we hear echoes of St. Paul speaking of those who, claiming to be wise, become fools. Thus, with current calls for 'justice' we have witnessed the foolishness of a Nobel Laureate being forced to resign his university post because he expressed the thought that he found it easier to work with men than women.[13] Similarly, we feel for the plight of women, alarmed by the idea that men who insist they are women must be allowed to use female washrooms.[14] This is the kind of foolishness that ensues when societal norms are discarded.

But more, when children are taught not to engage in discerning thought which reasons 'this is good but that is better,' they are wide open to manipulation and brainwashing by totalitarian ideology. Their mental defences have been breached. Good is evil and evil is good (Is. 5:20).

But by contrast to the perverse thinking engineered by Social Justice advocates, ordinary people tend to have a default setting of what we call 'common sense'. For example, they can see that men are not women. They know that only male-female marriage can produce a natural family. In fact, 'common sense' goes back to creation and matches a Christian worldview.

The God who makes sense

The Lord Jesus, the Word of God (Jn. 1:1), is the true light that lights every human being who comes into the world (Jn. 1:9). The one through whom the world was made is the one who alone makes sense of the world. So it is that the basic tenets of Christian theology lead us to the viability of human thought and rationality. Let's briefly sketch this out under seven headings.

One: The existence of God

Genesis 1:1 guarantees the existence of truth. Whether or not we are able to find it, the truth exists, and the truth about any and

---

13   See *The Guardian*, 13 June 2015
14   See for example, *The Guardian*, 3 October, 2018

every person and event, exists in the mind of God. This means that, contrary to the assumptions of postmodernism, the pursuit of truth is a worthwhile exercise. But to deny the existence of God can be likened to rubbing out the axes of truth and error, right and wrong, on the graph of life. We are left with self as our only point of reference and not knowing where we are or which direction is which. Hence the confused state of our benighted world.

Two: The faithfulness of God

Lamentations 3:23 means that God does not change and his truth is therefore not in constant flux. He and the laws which he built into creation are reliable. What was true yesterday will be true tomorrow. Once truth is established, we do not have to constantly rethink everything.

Three: The image of God in humanity

Genesis 1:26-27 guarantees that we were made with the ability to engage with the real world. Though we may not know the whole truth, as God does, for we are finite not infinite, yet we can know true things because we are like God. We are made, in the astronomer Kepler's words, to 'think God's thoughts after him'. Again, this makes for a 'common sense' approach to life.

Four: The revelation of God

God is the first speaker (Gen. 1:3). This means that language is not simply a human construct. God speaks to man and he can understand (Gen. 2:16–17). Language can truly express reality. Adam's naming of the animals (Gen. 2:19) was significant not futile. Adam's recognizing his wife as a woman (Gen. 2:23), equal with him as a human being in God's image but different from him, means that he is able to recognize norms and categories which God has built into the world and has himself differentiated (Gen. 1:27). He can trust his senses. Evidence means something and is not to be ignored. What is more, this means that we can share truth as human beings. Indeed, without shared common truth, democracy itself becomes impossible and meaningless.

Five: *Our sin against God*

The Fall (Gen. 3:11) has not only meant that our world is now fallen and not as God originally made it, but it has corrupted us as human beings. We have become sinners in need of salvation. There are now deep injustices in the world. But those things can only be put right by returning to God's ways, not by rejecting the structures which God built into the world. Sin has made us all prone to selfishness and being self-righteous. Common sense tells us that we can't simply divide the world into 'good' people and 'bad' people as Social Justice tends to do – those 'for' and those 'against'. We all have our faults, weaknesses and blind spots.

Six: *The love of God*

This is a constant theme in Scripture. God is love and he expects us to love one another (Mk. 12:29-31). God has shown us what real love is through the death of Jesus for our sins (1 Jn. 3:16). But Social Justice theory paints a contrary and very bleak picture of human relationships. It would see every human interaction in terms of power and manipulation on the part of one person or the other or both. Every relationship is viewed through cynical eyes. There is no room for true altruism and love or even real romance. Under this regime our world is becoming a grim and joyless place. But common sense tells us that there are such things as love and kindness which are not to be deliberately misunderstood and denigrated but valued. The Good Samaritan was not on an ego trip when he helped the man who had been beaten up (Lk. 10:30-37). In fact he was expressing something of the love of God.

Seven: The power of God

This shows us that there is such a thing as the benevolent use of power. God used his power to create us, sustain us and save us. It is good power (Ps. 145:6–7). Social Justice requires an absolute equality for everyone and sees all imbalances of power as detrimental. But God has built structure and authority into the world for mutual blessing. He has given authority within the family and the state. The strong and those in authority are meant to use their power for the good of those who are weaker. The weak can rejoice in this. For example, we are so glad when doctors and nurses who have knowledge and powers beyond us tend to our needs. And the medics can feel worthwhile and find joy in service and being useful to others. And indeed, those medics, who are weak in another area, say having no ability in the area of auto maintenance, can be blessed when the mechanic, who perhaps they treated in hospital, fixes their car. This is true and helpful diversity.

All this and more gives the foundation for a common sense view of life.[15] It is good for Christians to know that in the problems we are likely to face in coming years common sense is on our side.

---

15   For a more thorough explanation of how Christianity provides the basis for logical thought and a common sense view of the world see, for example, Francis Schaeffer, 'He is there and he is not silent', in *The Complete Works of Francis Schaeffer*, Crossway Books, 1982, volume 1, page 275.

5: How can pastors help the churches?

Our world faces a number of problems which require global solutions. The ongoing crisis with respect to man-made climate change springs to mind. Again, the calamity of poverty in many countries while the rich continually get richer, can only be thoroughly addressed through worldwide action.[16] We think too of the recent coronavirus pandemic which swept across the planet. And the Social Justice movement does its best to piggy-back on such issues and to present itself as a 'new morality' which will be part of the answer to such diffculties and therefore should be adopted across the world.

But while it will engage itself in various countries for things like LGBT rights and condemn national governments where laws oppose such lifestyles, at the same time its advocates strive to de-platform and silence those who disagree with their own agenda. Social Justice only wants freedom for people to say what it wants said. This is a classic mark of totalitarianism.

Trouble coming

Indeed, China has begun to use methods, very like those we have outlined, to control its vast population and conform it to their current Communist ideology. There is a huge machinery of surveillance and

16 Interestingly, the Social Justice movement rarely seems to have directly addressed the subject of poverty.

a system of 'social credit' in which individuals are assigned points based on what is known of their behaviour. Those who fail to conform are not even allowed to ride on public transport. Churches are kept under surveillance. Many have to meet secretly. Pastors are arrested. In China it is now illegal to teach the gospel to children.

Social Justice is not old-fashioned Communism. However, a number of thinkers have already identified it as 'cultural Marxism' and, as we have seen, it is in close cahoots with the surveillance giants of the internet.[17]

Maybe such things could never happen in the West. But maybe they could. However, what is certain is that the church will not be helped by simply sticking its head in the sand and carrying on pretending that we still live in the 1980s. We don't. Like it or not the world is changing and Christians must wake up.

As this movement gains increasing control over our culture, trouble inevitably awaits faithful Christians and churches. Without being alarmist, we should be asking ourselves what pastors and preachers can do to prepare God's people for the future? This question is particularly pressing in the West. In other parts of the world the church knows what it is like to be persecuted. We don't.

Forward thinking leaders

Understandably, Christian leaders like to plan for the growth of the church. But the time has come to think how the churches can survive and prosper in a much harsher cultural and spiritual climate than we are used to.

Pastors must, of course, think these things through for themselves, but let me suggest a seven-fold package of biblical ideas

---

17   See for example Melvin Tinker, *That Hideous Strength: How the West was Lost – the cancer of cultural Marxism in the church and the world*, EP books, 2018

we might want to get our churches to take more seriously than they have done before.

One: Alerting the congregation

The apostle Paul warns of 'terrible times' for the church in the last days (2 Tim. 3:1). He describes the kind of society from which such troubles for the church will emerge, and what he describes looks very like our society (2 Tim. 3:2-5). During such periods every true Christian will face persecution (2 Tim. 3:12). Our congregations may find it diffcult to receive such teaching. It will not make you popular. But pastor, be brave enough to alert your people to what is going on and what is likely to come – because you care for their souls.

Two: Prizing truth

False teachings, both secular and religious, influence society during these predicted 'terrible times'. Those behind the mischief are described as unable to acknowledge the truth (2 Tim. 3:7), and as those who 'oppose the truth' (2 Tim. 3:8). All totalitarian systems are built on seemingly convenient lies.

Before all else, the job of the Christian is to prize the truth. Therefore we must continue to teach the Bible to the church. And all truth is God's truth, not just the gospel, because he is Lord of all. Living by truth is the first way to resist all enforced ideologies, including Social Justice. Christians need to be reminded of this and what it means in practice.

Three: Teaching about persecution

Because it is many years since Christians in the West have suffered real persecution, pastors and preachers have tended to neglect this area of Bible teaching. But it is time for pastors to dust it off and put such teaching unashamedly front and centre once again. In particular, it would be good to focus on what the Lord Jesus himself taught in passages like Mark 13:9–13 and John 15:18–16:4. The book of Revelation was partly written with the intent of preparing Christians for persecution. Again, 1 Peter was penned for persecuted churches with the exhortation that they should not be surprised at the fiery trial they are suffering, as though something strange were happening to them (1 Pet. 4:12).

Four: Going underground

Up until now we have been understandably very keen for our churches to have a profile in our communities and to be known by everyone. But when persecution comes often the church needs to go underground and meet in secret (1 Kgs. 17:2–3; Mk. 13:14–15). It is time to think through what that could look like in today's society. How can you pastor an underground church where it is diffcult for people to meet? How does a pastor continue to teach the flock under such circumstances? The time may well come when we need to rethink our church's engagement with the internet which makes surveillance of our activities so comparatively simple.

Five: Small groups and families

Personal support is best done in small groups where people are able to talk truthfully. Even large churches know this. If persecution comes in some form, not only do small groups draw less attention but Christians will need the close support that small groups can give. The 'one another' commands of the New Testament come into their own via intimate fellowship.[18] Confidentiality is key. Is it time for leaders to be strengthening the small group life of their churches?

And it is worth bearing in mind that, historically, under persecution, sometimes Christians have only been able to 'meet' in their own families. Is it time to reinvigorate family worship among Christians? 'As twenty-first-century Christians, we are driven back by a militant intolerance of Bible truth and those who adhere to it. Maybe a time will come where family culture will be the only place where we preserve gospel truth and pass on the baton'.[19]

Six: Taking opportunities

Under circumstances where the gospel is publicly suppressed, evangelism has to be personal evangelism. It is interesting that the NT speaks to ordinary Christians in terms of taking opportunities rather than making opportunities to share the good news of Jesus (Eph. 5:15; Col. 4:5; 1 Pet. 3:15). A new understanding of this and how to sense what the Holy Spirit is doing as we look to make Christ known individually would be helpful.

Seven: Praying always

When the early church first began to suffer persecution, their immediate response was to pray (Acts 4:23–24; Acts 12:5). As we move into more diffcult times, pastors cannot allow themselves and their people to be comparative strangers to the place of prayer. Prayer is the church's mighty secret weapon in times of trouble.

---

18 Hereafter, 'New Testament' is abbreviated to 'NT'.

19 Ann Benton, *The Fruitful Home: creating a gospel culture for family life*, 10Publishing, 2019, page 125.

We believe that Jesus will always have the ultimate victory. His church will be built despite all that the 'gates of hell' can contrive (Mt. 16:18). So, we face the future in faith. But we should prepare and use the means which our Master has put at our disposal.

6: The Lord encourages us

The prospect of persecution is, of course, not something we should relish. In a sense, I really hope I'm totally wrong about the consequences of 'soft totalitarianism' for the church which have been sketched out in this book.

However, if some kind of crackdown on Bible Christians and faithful churches is coming our way in the next few years then we need to remember that we are not on our own. The Lord Jesus has said, 'I am with you always, to the very end of the age' (Mt. 28:20). That includes the twenty-first century. He has promised his people, 'Never will I leave you; never will I forsake you' (Heb. 13:5) and our response can be legitimately to say to ourselves, 'The Lord is my helper; I will not be afraid. What can mere mortals do to me?' (Heb. 13:6).

The Lord and the Spirit

Moreover, the Lord promises special help for his people when they face criticism and threats from the courts. The advocates of Social Justice appear so adept in their use of words and their political know how. But we will know the Lord's presence with us (2 Tim. 4:16–17). Here is a promise of our Lord Jesus Christ which we can hold on to: 'Whenever you are arrested and brought to trial, do not worry beforehand about what to say. Just say whatever is given you at the time, for it is not you speaking, but the Holy Spirit' (Mk 13:11).

We can rely on the Lord to give us the strength we need at the time we need it. Here's an example: John Lennox, until recently a professor of mathematics at Oxford University, used to travel behind the Iron Curtain in the days of Communism. He writes of meeting a man who had been detained in a Siberian labour camp for the crime of teaching children from the Bible.

> He described to me [says Lennox] how he had seen things no man should see. I listened, thinking how little I really knew about life, and wondering how I would have fared under his circumstances. As if he read my thoughts he suddenly said: "You couldn't cope with that could you?" Embarrassed, I stumbled out something like: "No, I'm sure you are right." He grinned and said: "Nor could I! I was a man who fainted at the sight of his own blood, let alone that of others. But what I discovered in the labour camp was this: God does not help us face theoretical situations but real ones. Like you, I couldn't imagine how one could cope in the Gulag. But once there I found that God met me, exactly as Jesus promised his disciples when he was preparing them for victimization and persecution."[20]

Blessing amid the trouble

Not only will the Lord sustain us but we often find that amid troubles, God's people know deep spiritual enrichment. So it's not all bad. We think of Paul and Silas singing praises to God while in prison in Philippi (Acts 16:25). And the Lord intervened in a remarkable way bringing about the conversion of the jailer and his family.

So though coming days could be frightening and dangerous, let's keep things in perspective. The Lord Jesus said, 'Blessed are you

20 *Against the tide: the inspiration of Daniel in an age of relativism*, by John Lennox, Monarch 2017, page 150-151

when people insult you, persecute you and falsely say all kinds of evil against you because of me. Rejoice and be glad, because great is your reward in heaven, for in the same way they persecuted the prophets who were before you' (Mt. 5:11–12).

Part Four: Gender Confusion

A briefing for Bible Christians

Introduction

Is there a difference between our sex and our gender? What's wrong with same-sex marriage? What's the problem with physical intimacy between people of the same sex, as long as it is consensual? Is there a spectrum of genders with male and female not the only options? Can a boy be genuinely trapped in a girl's body? Is the best solution for a person who thinks like that about themselves to have surgery?

These are some of the questions which face Christians and the churches now.

Urgency

And such questions come with an urgency which we may not have realised yet.

Back in 1934, the Oxford academic, J.D. Unwin published his book *Sex and Culture* (Oxford University Press). His work investigated the correlation between a society's level of sexual restraint and its stability and achievements. He found that where chastity and (old fashioned) monogamy prevailed, society flourished. But, according to Unwin, once a nation becomes too prosperous it tends to embrace an increasingly liberal stance towards sexual activity and relationships. This in turn leads to a loss of society's cohesion (through such things as family breakdown or failure to form families) accompanied by a dissipation of a society's momentum and sense of purpose. Social 'entropy' is accelerated, thereby diminishing its creativity and energy. The society begins to unravel.

Unwin's studies led him to believe that the full effect of this decline is not realised until the third generation. Change takes root slowly in the first generation, becomes more normalised in the second, its full effect only emerging in the third generation.

Interestingly, if we equate a generation with around 20-30 years and locate the beginning of the West's sexual revolution in the 1960s with the advent of the contraceptive pill, then if Unwin is correct, our society is just entering the period of full societal breakdown.

Not the time to compromise

Well, the indicators of a society that has lost its way seem to be all around us, don't they? And now is not the time for the church to be compromising with this stuff, but to understand what is going on and give a compassionate and clear lead.

In this brief part I want to try to give us a handle on some of this by looking at a number of different aspects regarding the current challenge of *gender confusion*. All I can do here is to give some notes and possible pointers for our thinking. We will glimpse the theology, the history and the psychology of gender confusion.

1: A theology of gender confusion

Clear Bible theology will help us to think straight about complex issues and have the mind of Christ. Though we may live in a rapidly changing world, the Bible is still God's word and Jesus assured us that though heaven and earth may pass away, his words would never pass away or become irrelevant (Lk. 21:33).

The Lord Jesus, when questioned about marriage, divorce and sexual relationships was unashamed to refer back to the book of Genesis in order to give his answer. He said, 'At the beginning the Creator "made them male and female", and said, "for this reason a man will leave his father and mother and be united to his wife ..."' (Mt. 19:4–5). He uses two quotations. They are from Genesis 1:27 and Genesis 2:24.

Notice, *first*, according to Jesus we are created beings, made by the Creator God. That is so important in our thinking. We did not emerge by chance. Nor did we make ourselves. Though we have great dignity as human beings made in the image of God, yet we are only creatures not gods.

Second, note that Jesus says that human beings are made by God male and female. Therefore, male and female are not social constructs nor simply a matter of our own inner consciousness. They are God's design indicated by the different biology he endowed us with.

Genesis 2 makes it particularly clear that male and female are rooted in the physical attributes God gave us. With regard to Adam, in Genesis 2:7 we read, 'the LORD God formed a man from the dust of the ground and breathed into his nostrils the breath of life, and the man became a living being'. The word for man and Adam are the same. But the indication here is that Adam, made out of the dust of the earth, was male even before God breathed life into him and gave him consciousness. His maleness was rooted in what he had been made physically.

We find a similar truth regarding Eve. We read in Genesis 2:22-23 the following: 'Then the LORD God made a woman from the rib he had taken out of the man, and he brought her to the man. The man said, "This is now bone of my bones and flesh of my flesh; she shall be called 'woman' for she was taken out of man."'

Adam's designating of Eve as 'woman' came as God brought her to him and he first saw her. Based on her physicality Adam saw she was both like him and different from him and called her 'woman'. This, as far as we can see from the text, was before Eve had ever spoken to Adam or expressed anything to him about how she thought of herself.

These days many people speak in terms of our sex being what we are physically and our gender being how we think of ourselves. But Genesis indicates that we should take our cue of how we think of ourselves from our physical attributes.

So biblically we are created beings, male and female and our biological sex and our gender are synonymous. Precious because made in God's image, that's who we are. And that's how Jesus saw us.

Since the Fall there are now aberrations physically from this pattern. These disorders of sex development (DSDs) are very infrequent – and those folk need special care and consideration –

but the 'created male and female' is still the overall rubric – as the whole science of biology, not just human biology, tells us.[1]

Where are we today?

Given this Bible background here are three considerations to help us understand where we are now.

One: In a secular society, feeling good eventually takes precedence over common sense.

Practical atheism is one of the axioms of modern life for 'intelligent' people. When people no longer believe in God, they turn in upon themselves. They become 'lovers of pleasure rather than lovers of God' (2 Tim. 3:4). There is nothing else to live for. And because it brings such powerfully enjoyable emotions, this often comes down to sex and sexual desire.

A godless culture's prioritising 'feel good' and sex is taught throughout Scripture. Jeremiah describes how illicit passion consumes those who have turned away from the Lord: 'They are well-fed, lusty stallions, each neighing for another man's wife,' (Jer. 5:8). Paul describes how, when people reject God, he gives 'them over in the sinful desires of their hearts to sexual impurity,' (Rom. 1:24) and in a parallel verse, 'having lost all sensitivity [to God], they

---

1 DSD, or disorders of sex development are often referred to as 'intersex'. This term is misleading and some who have DSDs consider it an offensive term. It implies there is 'another' sex, or there are other things between the binary divide of male and female. DSDs are numerous in type, but rare to occur. Particular kinds of DSD can only appear in a biological male, and other kinds only in females. Therefore, DSDs reinforce the binary nature of biological sex. They are also not something to 'identify as', which is why many people who speak up about having a DSD don't like being included in the LGBTQIA+ listing. It's a medical condition, not an identity.

have given themselves over to sensuality so as to indulge in every kind of impurity, and they are full of greed' (Eph. 4:19). God gives them over – they give themselves over.

With the priority of 'feel good' the internal, personal world of individuals takes precedence over the external. The subjective trumps the objective. So, we get this dislocation between gender and sex. What I am biologically (male?) is of secondary importance, if I feel more comfortable, especially sexually, as a female – because feeling positive, satisfying my desires is my life – it is who I am. But, thinking themselves to be wise, they become fools (Rom. 1:22). Our world has an objective reality whether we *like* it or not and to pretend otherwise brings tragedy.

Two: Behind this attitude to life is the Satan's original lie – 'You will be like God'.

Adam and Eve were lured into disobeying God's command not to eat the forbidden fruit by Satan's promise of deity (Gen. 3:5).

Genesis 1 tells us that God is the Creator, Genesis 1:1. But the contemporary world replies with a sinful, rebellious 'No'. 'I shall be my own creator – I will decide what I shall be, and what is good, what is right for me – no-one else, and especially not God'. 'I will be God'. You can be whatever you want to be (I'm sure you've heard that kind of thing) and it finds particular expression in the ethos of gender confusion. 'I will decide if I'm male or female or something else'.

Given this way of thinking, the world is now not so much a given within which I am to operate – but a lump of playdough that I can make into whatever I want. I will be whatever I want to be. And of course, the advances in some modern technologies can appear to reinforce that idea. CGI (Computer Generated Images) means I can create a total fantasy world of weird creatures and whatever on screen – and why shouldn't I become one? Whatever the problems of me following through on choosing my own gender and sexual preferences – I'm sure advances in modern surgery and medicine can overcome them. This is the current *hubris* of many of our contemporaries.

But the promise 'You will be like God' was a lie, and if you read Abigail Shrier's book *Irreversible Damage: Teenaged Girls and the Transgender Craze*[2] you will see that is still the case as young teenagers have wrecked their lives through surgery and testosterone therapy they later deeply regretted. And given the current politically correct ideology, no-one, not even health professionals dared challenge them – because people must be free to be whatever they want to be. This is all terribly wrong, but our hearts go out to those caught up in these things.

Three: The perpetration of this original lie from the garden of Eden (and this is speculative) just may signal the beginning of Satan's little season, 'which deceives the nations in the four corners of the earth' which we read about in Revelation 20.

This whole gender confusion ideology linked with the so-called Woke agenda of 'being alert to layers of "oppression" in society'[3] has taken such deep root so quickly, and made such inroads even into the church itself, that I think we must take seriously very difficult times ahead for the faithful church.

---

2   Abigail Shrier, *Irreversible Damage: Teenaged Girls and the Transgender Craze*, Swift Books, 2021
3   Noelle Mering, *Awake, not Woke*,Tan books, 2021, page 9

2: A history of gender confusion

We must ask a question. Why has all this gender confusion come to the fore now? Why wasn't this so well-known and accepted in earlier centuries? Surely human beings have always been sinful – so what has happened to nurture the sexual revolution and its accompanying gender confusion into the open so powerfully? Well, for sure, this has not come out of the blue.

There is much that could be said, including reference to the decline of belief in Christianity in the West and the development of digital technology and the internet which means ideas can spread across the globe more quickly. But there is a story linked to the changes in people's outlook which does explain quite a lot. The story goes something like this – in very simplified form.

Marx and sex

For reasons that will become obvious we take Karl Marx, materialist and atheist, as our starting point. With nineteenth century thoughts of evolution and the progress of society in the back of his mind Marx (1818-1883) held the idea of the upward climb of society through revolution. Seeing the wealth of the aristocracy and factory owners and the grinding poverty of most workers (almost enslavement) his understanding was that through a series of violent confrontations, societies could be vastly improved for the majority of people. He felt his calling was to stir the masses to overthrow the *status quo*.

One obstacle to this was religion. Faith can encourage people to accept their circumstances now and put their hope in a better life to come. This would not help Marx agitate the workers to action. So Christ and the church, he thought, lulled a population into sitting on their hands and doing nothing, and so became the enemy.

But the other obstacle he saw was that working people were willing to put up with difficult conditions, simply out of love for their families and their desire to provide for them. In this way family gave strength to Capitalism. Thus, the family too becomes the enemy. And what better way to undermine the family than representing marriage as an oppression and preaching sexual 'liberation'.

Here is a quote from the Catholic writer, Noelle Mering: 'Echoing earlier writings of Marx, Engels argued in *The Origin of the Family* that women ought to become liberated from the oppression of their husbands by entering ... the workforce. Marx and Engels laid the foundation for (the word) "patriarchy" as pejorative. Housework should be nationalized, they claimed, and children were to be raised not by parents but communally. Besides advancing the power of the (Communist) state, these changes would lead to more women being available for sex by removing their need for the support of a husband or the responsibility of child care.'[4]

Twentieth century

This 'sexual revolution' strategy came increasingly to the forefront in the early twentieth century. Under the influence of Freud, the father of psychoanalysis, through the so-called 'Frankfurt School' (which moved to America in the 1930s as they fled Hitler) this became enormously influential. People like Wilhelm Reich (1930s)

---

4   Noelle Mering, *Awake, Not Woke: A Christian Response to the Cult of Progressive Ideology*, Tan Books, 2021, pages 33-34 (brackets mine, JB)

and later Herbert Marcuse (1960s) pushed radical ideas about sex. It promoted the undermining of family. Making men lecherous through pornography, for example, engenders distrust of them in their wives and despising of them in their children – families fall apart, so get pornography out there for the revolution.

All this was in the intellectual background as the rather naïve 'Flower Power' 'Free Love' Generation of the 1960s emerged – with the pill and legal abortion. In 1960 the book, *Lady Chatterley's Lover*, D. H. Lawrence's sexually explicit novel, was adjudged by the UK courts to be suitable to be sold in bookshops. And around this point the sexual revolution begins to break away from its roots in cultural Marxism to have a life of its own as godless 'feel good' society validates lust. 'Life is for living', they would say – by which they meant enjoy yourself with as few trammels as possible.

It was in the late 1960s that homosexuality began to raise its profile especially after the Sexual Offences Act of 1967. Homosexual acts were made legal so long as this took place between consenting adults. Obviously, from a Christian point of view homosexual relationships are inimical to the ordinary family.

The whole homosexual outlook opens the door to confusing gender and it moved very quickly from being 'the love that dare not speak its name' to the centre of Western public life, especially through the repackaging advised in the 1990s by the book *After the Ball: How America will conquer its Fear and Hatred of Gays*, written by two advertising consultants with both psychiatric and public relations expertise. Basically the message was, play down the more gross, strident side of gay lifestyle and tell stories of lonely, middle-aged women who find companionship and sexual comfort in each other. Make it look cuddly and altruistic. And meanwhile 'fun' TV soaps like *Sex in the City* (produced by gay men it seems) – normalised all kinds of sexual activity and attitudes in the eyes of the public as they laughed along. (And meanwhile, these things were hardly mentioned in church and to preach from Scripture concerning such things was often frowned upon).

But all this was carrying the subtext that your sexual desires are the most important thing about you. Your sexual proclivities are your identity – who you really are and what your life is about.

LGBT

And, inevitably, it was not long before a community emerged saying 'I am not straight or gay, I am transgender'. This is who I am. And here we are into real gender confusion. Some people were saying, for example, 'I may have the body of a man, but I feel most comfortable thinking of myself as a woman. And to exclude me or marginalise me because of my sexual identity is an act of oppression'. Transgender had arrived. LGBT formed as a coalition. It now holds astonishing sway with its rainbow flags across the Western world.

But what is becoming increasingly obvious is that Lesbian, Gay and Transgender do not fit together. Many lesbians, for example, don't want transgender men among them. Both lesbian and gay outlooks are predicated upon the idea of binary sex. Trans and other outlooks are not. But, notice, the coalition is held together by their common rejection of God's created norms for sexual activity.

As an example of the tensions within the LGBT movement it was notable that in October 2022 the author of the famous *Harry Potter* books, J K Rowling, supported those protesting against the Scottish Parliament's gender recognition legislation which backed the idea that people should be able to self-identify as whatever sex they want. There would be no need for doctors' reports. Those who protested said that the law would undermine the safety of women-only spaces (like female toilets) and would make the most vulnerable women less safe. As part of the protest, Rowling wore a T-shirt with wording calling Scotland's then First Minister, Nicola Sturgeon, 'a destroyer of women's rights.' Who knows how all this will play out in the long run?

Agents and victims

But once you begin to see this story of sexual 'liberation' and its consequences – rooted in cultural Marxism and the attack on the family – you realise that there is at least an element of our society being not just rebellious, but being manipulated into gender confusion – especially through the immense presence of a hard-line LGBT community on the internet and social media – ready to shout down and deride anyone who questions where all this is leading.

And, though many ties have been cut with cultural Marxism, nevertheless, in true Marxist style, they are ready to deny what is fact – to sacrifice truth if it does not conform with 'the party line'.

Writing in *The Spectator* recently the journalist Mary Wakefield began an article titled *Parents must resist Stonewall's gospel* saying:

> I think it's becoming horribly apparent to parents of every political persuasion that we can't sit out the culture wars ... It (is) impossible to ignore the fact that gender activism these days isn't about gay rights or even trans rights, it's not about being inclusive, it's about presenting utter nonsense as plain fact.[5]

And what she had in mind were such things as the propaganda that no-one is born male or female. She asks the obvious question, 'If there's no such thing as biological sex, why does any child need to transition at all?' Thinking themselves to be wise they have become fools.

---

5   *The Spectator*, 16 July 2022, page 23

3: A psychology of gender confusion

Some people take the transgender route having suffered rape or sexual abuse, thinking that changing gender might be a safeguard against that happening to them again. We should have great sympathy for such folk. Far more sinister, however, at the other end of the spectrum, there seems to be evidence that some drug companies are promoting trans because basically those who undergo surgery and hormone therapy become patients for life. They become people needing all kinds of pharmaceuticals for years and years. If the reports are right, this is simply about preying on people in order to make money.

Gender dysphoria

Now we need to be clear before we go any further that there is a genuine medical/psychological condition known as gender dysphoria or formerly 'gender identity disorder'. It has been known for many years and follows a known pattern. It is characterised by the presence of severe and persistent discomfort with one's biological sex. This typically begins to manifest itself in early childhood – ages 2 to 4 – though it may grow more severe in adolescence. In most cases – I have heard 70% to 90% quoted - childhood gender dysphoria resolves itself with time.

Note however that historically it was present in a very tiny proportion of the population – we are talking roughly 0.01% –

and almost exclusively in boys. Abigail Shrier writes, 'Before 2012 there was no scientific literature on girls ages 11 to 21 ever having developed gender dysphoria at all.'[6] But for some reason, now many teenaged girls are identifying as trans.

My main concern today is this: Why this sudden explosion of youngsters, especially girls, claiming to be transgender? What's going on? I realise there are other age groups and much more to consider but that's what we are going to focus on here.

It is worth just stopping to note this: the 0.01% figure which is quoted is equivalent to 1 in 10,000 children. If the average secondary school had 2,000 pupils (and that's a high estimate), you would expect to find just one youngster in five schools suffering from this problem. But that is, evidently, far from the case at present. It seems currently that almost every school in the country has children who are presenting as trans. There are girls dressing as boys and boys dressing as girls in many classrooms. Why?

To put my cards on the table this looks like a craze. In fact it gives signs even of being something of a cult – stirred up by LGBT activists and others with access to young people via social media/internet.

Considerations

Here are some of the reasons as to why I think this.

Firstly, teenaged years are classically difficult for young people as they struggle in the move from childhood to adulthood and trying to 'find out who they are'.

Often, they feel awkward, unsure of themselves, sometimes despondent, powerless, and unhappy. As an expression of these

---

6   Abigail Shrier, *Irreversible Damage*, Introduction, page xxvii

kinds of inner tensions, over recent years we have had a succession of unhelpful 'epidemics' among young people.

In my early years as a pastor, it was the terrible scourge of anorexia. Many teenagers starved themselves seeing themselves as being too fat. It then moved on to self-harm. Youngsters have deliberately cut their arms and let blood as a habit. These are expressions of youngsters, at some level, not liking themselves. And the transgender epidemic appears to be in the same line of things. There are voices out there in society telling teenagers, 'you are feeling like you don't like yourself and don't belong – you are unhappy – it's because you are the wrong sex...you need to change gender.' That is the powerful message out there, seemingly so convincing, which speaks to the teenagers' vulnerabilities.

Secondly, this 'outbreak' of gender confusion among teenagers (having never shown any signs of gender dysphoria in their earlier years) really does not fit the known pattern.

I have said there are rare genuine cases of gender dysphoria of which we need to be mindful but something else is going on here in a trend that doesn't look like the genuine article. And we know the power of the internet especially in the lives of young people. Just recently there has been the inquest on Molly Russell, who killed herself at the age of 14 back in 2017 after viewing material online about self-harm, suicide and depression on platforms such as Instagram and Pinterest. Molly's story has provided fresh impetus for big-tech companies to be more closely regulated. There is an awful lot online about becoming transgender, what surgery is required, what drugs to get hold of, and how to handle parents who might disapprove. To suggest this is having no effect on young people is extremely naïve.

It is worth noting the words of the coroner from Molly Russell's inquest. He said,

> Molly appeared a normal healthy girl who was flourishing at school. However, Molly had become depressed, a common condition affecting children of this age. This then worsened into depressive illness. Molly subscribed to a number of online sites ... Some of these sites were not safe as they allowed access to adult content that should not have been available for a 14-year-old child to see. The way that the platforms operated meant that Molly had access to images, video clips and text concerning self-harm, suicide or that were otherwise negative or depressing in nature. The platform operated in such a way, using algorithms, as to result ... in binge periods of images some of which were provided without Molly requesting them. In some cases, the content was particularly graphic, tending to portray self-harm and suicide as an inevitable consequence of a condition that could not be recovered from. The sites normalised her condition, focusing on a limited and irrational view without any counterbalance of normality. It is likely that the above material viewed by Molly, already suffering with a depressive illness and vulnerable due to her age affected her mental health in a negative way and contributed to her death in a more than minimal way.[7]

If online sites can contribute in a 'more than minimal way' to a teenager's suicide they are just as likely to have a big effect on youngsters wondering about changing sex.

Thirdly, the idea that this outbreak is not genuine is also backed up on the ground.

I spoke to a parent whose children go to school in London. The school caters for girls presenting as boys and vice versa in the

---

7   *The Independent*, 30th September 2022

way they dress, and it provides support for such children. But, and here's the crucial thing, the school does not 'celebrate' their chosen gender. They support but will not have a fuss made. The dopamine of applause for what the children are doing is denied. The school's experience is that after a couple of years most of these children stop saying they are transgender and just revert to being boys or girls according to what they are physically. So again, what is happening doesn't look genuine.

What are they thinking?

Why would children choose this path in the first place? What's the psychology here? At least four things seem to be going on.

1. The teenaged years, as we have said, are a struggle as young people move towards adulthood. At the back of their minds they are asking themselves, 'will I make the grade?' They are anxious. But remember how today's society works. To become a member of a marginalized/oppressed group is to gain victimhood. The thought is something like this: 'If I'm a victim then people will not expect so much of me – or if they do, they put themselves in the wrong'. So, this affords a way of self-protection. Here's a quote from a therapist writing for the Gender Exploratory Therapy Association[8]: 'In my ... work with mothers of teens ... I am a frequent second-hand witness to children who, seeking to avoid developmental demands of approaching independence, cling to their frailties.' Well,

---

8   Lisa Marchiano, 'Collision with Reality: What Depth Psychology Can Teach Us about Victimhood Culture and Teen Anxiety', Gender Exploratory Therapy, https://genderexploratory.com/2021/04/30/example-post-2/, accessed 15 February 2023

encouraging young people to become transgender gives an open door for them into frailty and victimhood.

2. The teenaged years, as youngsters seek to move towards standing on their own two feet as people, are also famously the years of rebellion against parents – who have got it wrong about everything. And the whole gender confusion thing and rejection of binary sex is a convenient stick with which to beat parents and to tell them they don't understand anything. We've all been there in our time as teenagers.

3. Add to that the need for teenagers to find their own community – separate from their parents – and peer group pressure to conform to what their friends are saying is cool and right. This too, of course, is a strong influence. And at present transgender is seen as cool.

4. It is also worth thinking about what has happened in recent years around gender stereotyping. In times gone by, we were rightly warned away from thinking that every man had to be macho and every woman a painted doll. In Scripture we find for example that some males were great warriors, like David's mighty men (2 Sam. 23:8-39), but others, like say Bezalel, the maker of the Tabernacle would have loved a craft shop (Ex. 31:1-6). But that did not make Bezalel any less a man than say, Joab the general. Or again think of Peter the brawny Galilean fisherman compared with Paul the academic who was good at needlework (Acts 18:3). There is a similar spectrum of personalities and skills among Bible women too (for example, Lk 10:38-42). The Bible tells us to beware of thinking too rigidly about what makes a male or a female. But these days the LGBT movement has often adopted and misused male and female

stereotypes. Boys are told that if they like sewing and cooking instead of football they must be gay. Girls are told that if they are more interested in cars and motorbikes than in going shopping for the latest fashions, they must be transgender or something similar. This kind of misguided 'logic' can get into the minds of teenagers and lead them astray.

If what we have proposed makes sense, then the conclusion is that it is not the dress or the bodies of teenagers that need changing, but rather their minds. For whatever reason they have been lured into a false way of thinking and they need, with kindness and support, to be led out of this and back to normality.

How families are affected

But meanwhile this kind of stuff is devastating families and family life. As an aside, it is worth remembering that the attack on the family, as biblically understood, is a theme that has run throughout our theological, historical and now our psychological sections of what we have been considering.

Mothers and fathers are in turmoil over what is happening to their children. Here is a piece from a website for (I think) US parents whose children have declared themselves transgender. A mother writes:

I have yet to meet a family, where one or both parents hasn't had a complete mental collapse following their child's announcement. Many have contemplated suicide, some seriously. Many parents, moms especially, have had to seek out mental health therapy and anti-depression or anti-anxiety drugs to cope with daily life, **in a world where there is a physical threat to their child AND all of society,**

seemingly, is aligned against them ... Strife between parents is also common, breaking down marriages and sibling relationships.[9]

Why are the parents losing it? Because in this movement, our confused kids, having been indoctrinated in the false belief that they can literally become the other sex and magically fix all of their problems, will seek out and easily obtain drugs that will chemically castrate them, break down their bones, and degrade their brain function. They can do this without any gatekeeping, without our permission, and without any real mental health screening or therapy.

The family unit is under siege, as parents wrangle with life or death decisions for their children, with no evidence-based information available, and tons of public pressure. Children are ... told to reject their loving parents and to trust outsiders that do not have their long-term best interests in mind ... It's appalling.[10]

The loving family is part of God's good in creation. But through gender confusion this gift of the Maker is both denigrated and sometimes destroyed.

So this is a huge thing facing parents and churches who stay close to biblical ideas of family life.

---

9   The bold type-face was part of the original
10   'Parental Mental Collapse', Parents with Inconvenient Truths about Trans (PITT), 19 September 2022, https://t.co/JPxR4HdyGU, accessed 15 February 2023

4: Facing Gender Confusion

What are we to do? How are Christians and churches to respond?

Parents

For parents with children who declare themselves transgender the message that seems to emerge from people's experiences is *first* that you must take control of your children's online access and cut them off, as far as you can, from transgender activists and those whose aim it is to destroy God's gift of family. We have already noted in the case of Molly Russell that the coroner emphasised the power of the internet over vulnerable and impressionable young people. This will need a straight but loving conversation with your teenagers about how the online world works and the artificial intelligence machines programmed to feed us things that will simply keep us glued to the screen. There is no concern here about what is best or healthy for viewers, but only what will keep us captivated.

The *Netflix* movie, *The Social Dilemma*, might be a good film for the whole family to watch together. It is a docu-drama, which includes tech experts from Silicon Valley sounding the alarm about the dangerous impact of social networking, which so-called 'Big Tech' companies use in an attempt to manipulate and influence us.

Second, as with the London school I mentioned, it is good for parents whose teenager has decided they are transgender or other to have an attitude of support for them as people but to refuse to celebrate or approve of their choice. What they are playing with is fire and is actually a huge mis-step in life. Don't make them into 'celebrities' for having made this choice. There must be love but there must also be truth (Eph. 4:15).

I know that this is more easily said than done – but that is round about where we have to land. And in all this, of course, pray.

Churches

For churches seeking to be faithful the message of love and truth is the same.

There must be a degree of love in the churches which sadly has rarely been seen in our day. One of factors which makes LGBT so attractive to some people is the strength of acceptance and kindness within that community. The church must more than match that with Christian love. In his book *Strange New World*, Carl Trueman writes the following:

> The reason they have moved from the margins to centre stage is intimately connected to the strong communities they formed while on the margins. This is why lamentation for Christianity's cultural marginalization, while legitimate, cannot be the sole response of the church to the current social convulsions she is experiencing. Lament for sure – we should lament that the world is not as it should be, as many of the Psalms teach us – but also organize. Become a community. By this, the Lord says, shall all men know that you are my disciples, by the love you have for each other, John 13:35. And that means community.[11]

However, there must also be truth as well as love. We must compassionately but without compromise stick to Scripture and biblical teaching on sex and gender. The kind of society which Paul

---

11 *Strange New World*, by Carl Trueman, Crossway, 2022, page 175

describes in 2 Timothy 3 as likely to occur in the last days is a society very like ours. People are described as being 'lovers of themselves' and 'lovers of pleasure rather than lovers of God' (v4). As we have seen earlier in this book this addiction to the self, this turning in on oneself, lies very much at the root of gender confusion as the felt needs of the self take precedence over reality.

But it is in just such a society as ours that Paul gives perhaps his most famous description of the Bible and the need for it, unaltered, to be preached.

> All Scripture is God-breathed and is useful for teaching, rebuking, correcting and training in righteousness, so that the servant of God may be thoroughly equipped for every good work. In the presence of God and of Christ Jesus, who will judge the living and the dead, and in view of his appearing and his kingdom, I give you this charge: Preach the word; be prepared in season and out of season; correct rebuke and encourage—with great patience and careful instruction. For the time will come when people will not put up with sound doctrine. Instead, to suit their own desires, they will gather round them a great number of teachers to say what their itching ears want to hear. They will turn their ears away from the truth and turn aside to myths. (2 Tim. 3:16–4:4)

We are to make communities of love and we are to preach the word. And we are to do this in hope. The faithful church can show the way to a lost world. Here are another couple of sentences from Carl Trueman's book:

> Many Christians talk of engaging the culture. In fact, the culture is most dramatically engaged by the church presenting it with another culture, another form of community, rooted in her liturgical worship practices and manifested in the loving community that exists both in and beyond the worship service. Many talk of the culture war between Christianity and secularism, and certainly the Bible uses martial language ... But

perhaps 'cultural protest' is a way of translating that idea into modern idiom ... The church protests the wider culture by offering a true vision of what it means to be a human being made in the image of God.[12]

And if J D Unwin was right – this is all extremely urgent.

---

12   Trueman, *Strange New World*, page 176

Works Cited

Benton, A. (2019). *The Fruitful Home: creating a gospel culture for family life*. 10Publishing.

Booker, C. (1980). *The Seventies*. Allen Lane.

Dreher, R. (2020). *Live Not By Lies: A manual for Christian dissidents*. Sentinel Books.

Figes, O. (2008). *The Whisperers: private life in Stalin's Russia*. Penguin.

Furedi, F. (2004). *Therapy Culture*. Routledge.

Haran, Y. N. (2011). *Sapiens: a brief history of human kind*. Harper-Collins.

Lennox, J. (2017). *Against the tide: the inspiration of Daniel in an age of relativism*. Monarch.

Lindsay, H. P. (2020). *Cynical Theories: how universities made everything about race, gender and identity – and why this harms everybody*. Swift Publishing.

MacAlpine, S. (2021). *Being the Bad Guys*. Good Book Company.

Mering, N. (2021). *Awake, Not Woke: A Christian Response to the Cult of Progressive Ideology*. Tan Books.

Murray, D. (2019). *The Madness of Crowds: Gender, Race and Identity.* Bloomsbury Continuum.

Petersen, J. B. (2018). *12 Rules for Life: an antidote to the chaos.* Allen Lane Publishing.

Schaeffer, F. (1982). *The Complete Works of Francis Schaeffer, volume 1.* Crossway Books.

Shrier, A. (2021). *Irreversible Damage: Teenaged Girls and the Transgender Craze.* Swift Books.

Storr, W. (2017). *Selfie: how the West became self-obsessed.* Picador Press.

Tinker, M. (2018). *That Hideous Strength: How the West was Lost – the cancer of cultural Marxism in the church and the world.* EP books.

Trueman, C. (2020). *The Rise and Triumph of the Modern Self: Cultural Amnesia, Expressive Individualism, and the Road to the Sexual Revolution.* Crossway.

Trueman, C. (2022). *Strange New World.* Crossway.

Zuboff, S. (2019). *The Age of Surveillance Capitalism: the fight for a human future at the new frontier of power.* Profile Books.

Pastors' Academy brings advanced theological study and
pastoral care to ministry life.
Pastors' Academy is part of London Seminary.

104 Hendon Lane London N3 3SQ
+44 (0)20 8346 7587
pastorsacademy@londonseminary.org

pastorsacademy.org

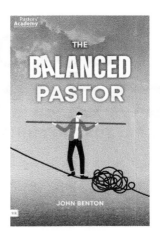

The Pastor with a Thorn in His Side
Edited by Stephen Kneale

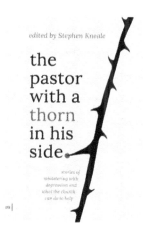

Depression is increasingly common. This is no less true for those in ministry. Many suffer with depression but feel unable to tell their churches about it.

This collection of real-life stories from pastors who have suffered with depression exists to encourage others in similar positions.

'Full of personal realism and practical, biblical wisdom.'
Mark Meynell